Spiritual Meteorology
Understanding the 7 Spirits of God

Russell Walden

DEDICATION

Special Thanks to Barbara Ann for her tireless assistance in this project

CHAPTER ONE: THE PREVAILING WINDS OF THE SPIRIT

According to Isa. 11:1-3 there are seven Spirits of God. The weather system that governs the climate of the earth is dominated by seven great rivers of wind called Jet Streams. Jesus told the Pharisees (Matt. 16:3) that studying the earth's weather would give insight into the kingdom of God and its workings among men. "The prince of the power of the air" (Luke 10:18) can be unseated and usurped by the power of God flowing through enlightened believers. Breakthrough in your life and transformation are possible and can be provoked, by posturing yourself to gather these winds of God: seeing these deployed in your life personally, in your church environment, and in your community. Toward that end, this book has been written.

There is an individual spiritual ecosystem that governs

every person's life. It can be influenced (and to some extent controlled), when you understand the forces at work and posture yourself to release the favor of God upon the area of your greatest need. Have you ever found yourself in a dry place in your Christian walk? Let the rains come. Have you experienced seasons of trial and difficulty? Has God ever rained his blessing down in your life? Or, perhaps there are storms of life bearing down on you. These are very familiar terms to most believers. Our language is replete with weather-related terminology used to describe our experiences in Christ.

The science of weather is called meteorology. There is a "meteorology" to the Christian experience and properly understood, will give you vast and deep insight into the affairs of life today and strong indication of what is ahead tomorrow. In fact, if the weather as a metaphor accurately describes the ebb and flow of life's experience, (and it does) then it follows that we should be able to reliably forecast the storms of life (just as the weatherman does on the 5 o'clock news) and do something to mitigate, if not diffuse, tomorrow's challenge altogether. The scriptures describe believers as kings unto God. Kings have kingdoms. They have power and authority portioned them from the Father. You can set your own season in God. You are not at the whim of chance and circumstance: Change is possible. In this book, you will explore how to cooperate with the process of God's blessing and breakthrough that is available to you.

Are you tempest-tossed in life? Are you having a flood of circumstances? These seasons can be predicted and planned. You can map the "pressure systems" that comprise the spiritual conditions of your life, and prepare for what is ahead. Through the knowledge found in this book, you will look into the heavenlies (the spiritual environment immediately around you), and by the gift of God, discern what tomorrow holds, and do something about it. You will know how to calm the storms and walk on the waters of adversity. It is time for you to understand and perceive what the Pharisees and unbelievers in Jesus' day could never understand. This is your activation time. The winds of God's favor are finding you, even now. Change is at hand and your blessing will be the end result!

Christians today use different kinds of imagery to describe their spiritual walk. A pastor inquiring into the well-being of a church member may hear something like this: "… pastor pray for me, I'm going through a stormy place in my walk with God right now." There are many weather-related and geographical terms believers instinctively use to describe and define their experiences in God. Have you heard of the mountaintop experience...? What about the valley? The scriptures are full of such metaphors intended to point you to the mysteries of God, which once understood, will show you how to influence these conditions.

Daniel Webster Whittle, a civil war veteran, wrote a hymn that expresses the blessings of God in meteorological or, weather-related terms. Whittle served in the 72nd Illinois Infantry and was wounded at Vicksburg. While recovering in the hospital, he retrieved from his haversack a New Testament his mother gave him. Out of boredom, he began to read, having no intention of converting or confessing Jesus as savior. He read straight through Matthew, Mark, Luke and John and found himself unmoved and unaffected.

However, a nurse who observed him reading the gospels, asked him to pray over a dying boy in a nearby ward.

Whittle was too embarrassed to admit to her that he was an unbeliever and agreed to go to the boy's side. The young man's wounds were obviously grievous and recovery was not a possibility. He would soon perish; it was plain to any observer, including the boy himself. Looking up from his deathbed, the dying lad begged Whittle to pray for his soul.

While Whittle didn't actually believe in God, at this point out of compassion for the dying boy, he began to pray. As Whittle prayed, the condition of his own soul became apparent to him. Suddenly, in great conviction he poured out his own heart to God, giving his life to Jesus as Lord and Savior. Then, as haltingly as he knew how, he prayed for the dying young man. Lifting his head after a few moments, he knew the boy was dead. From that moment on, Whittle was a changed man. He began to write and chronicle his love for Christ in verse and in several books on the subject of prayer. After the war, he (best known as Major Whittle) wrote over one hundred hymns. His most beloved hymn remains commonly used today, where hymnals are still employed. This hymn describes the spirit of God moving, in terms descriptive of the weather we witness every day:

> *"There shall be showers of blessing:*
>
> *This is the promise of love;*
>
> *There shall be seasons refreshing,*
>
> *Sent from the Savior above.*
>
> *Showers of blessing,*
>
> *Showers of blessing we need:*
>
> *Mercy drops round us are falling,*
>
> *But for the showers we plead."*

You can see the clouds of God and bring the beneficial rains of the Spirit to the parched plains of your experience. Certainly, as the song says, there are times when God's temporal and spiritual blessings are as abundant in your life, as spring rain. At other times, you may find yourself in a spiritual desert questioning all you know, or thought you knew about God and His word. These seasons of life are not intended to find you unawares. As with the natural weather, the spiritual weather of your life can be predicted and, in fact, anticipated – if you learn to look with the eye of God into your situation and circumstance.

You can predict your next season in God. In fact properly understood, you can set your own season in God and see the tides of adversity turned and breakthrough come. Just as Jesus was the master of winds and waves, He told us we would do likewise and even do greater things, according to John's gospel.

> *(John 14:12) "Verily, verily", I say unto you," He that believeth on me, the works that I do shall he do also, and greater [works] than these shall he do, because I go unto my Father."*

Jesus promised His disciples full disclosure of His heart and His teachings. He doesn't leave you out; nor does He hold back information or knowledge of what lies ahead (John 14:26). As He gave His life for us, so He gives (to us) of His understanding and knowledge, that the affairs and circumstances of life should not catch us unawares. Even in the Old Testament, God (through the prophet Amos) promised you that He would do nothing without involving you and informing you.

(Amos 3:7) Surely the Lord GOD will do nothing, but he revealeth his secret unto his servants the prophets.

You are not left out of the information loop concerning what is ahead for you. God's secrets and His insights are available and can be known, for those willing to hear as God hears and think as God thinks. It is important to realize that God speaks in His own language which requires effort and application on your part to decipher. If you expect the deep things of God to come to you like a Sunday school primer, you will be sadly disappointed. But the effort involved in divining the hidden things or even the secret things of God, are well worth the effort. You are an intelligent being capable of communicating with God, through His word, using capacities and capabilities inherent to the human condition. God does not want you to be uninformed in any way. The Apostle Paul put it this way:

(Rom. 1:13) Now I would not have you ignorant, brethren...

(Rom. 11:25) For I would not, brethren, that ye should be ignorant of this mystery...

(1 Cor. 10:1) Moreover, brethren, I would not that ye should be ignorant...

Ignorance is a possibility. Without applying yourself and turning away from the information distraction in your environment, you will be robbed of truths and teachings that could radically change your life for the good. God gave you a mind and He expects you to use it for your own spiritual betterment. One writer puts it this way: God didn't cut off your head when He took up residence in your heart. The rational mind can be at enmity against God and His ways, but it is possible to PUT ON the MIND OF CHRIST.

> *(Rom. 8:7) Because the carnal mind [is] enmity against God: for it is not subject to the law of God, neither indeed can be.*

> *(1 Cor. 2:16) For who hath known the mind of the Lord, that he may instruct him? But we have the mind of Christ.*

Toward that end, we present the information herein for your edification and enlightenment. The days ahead for you are not intended to be part of an inscrutable tomorrow. God is a God of disclosure; His very nature is expressed as LIGHT; He wants you to know. The keys to change and transformation are knowable and practical. Those who suggest otherwise are filtering their perceptions through a veil of fatalism and dead mysticism. God has nothing to hide and delights in disclosing Himself to you in substantive ways that will transform your life, your relationships, and bring you into your destiny.

> *(1 John 1:5) This then, is the message which we have heard of Him, declare unto you, that God is light and in Him is no darkness at all.*

God delights in revealing Himself to you and teaching you to look at life through the lens of His own infinite understanding. It is, in fact, the glory of God to conceal a matter, but the completion of that thought is, that it is the glory of kings to find it out (Prov. 25:2). You are one of the kings that verse speaks of (Rev. 1:6; 5:10).

> *(Prov. 25:2) [It is] the glory of God to conceal a thing: but the honor of kings [is] to search out a matter.*

(Rev. 1:6) And hath made us kings and priests unto God and his Father; to Him [be] glory and dominion forever, and ever, Amen.

(Rev. 5:10) And hast made us unto our God kings and priests, and we shall reign on the earth.

God has a voice. He will not leave you without answers for your life. He will show and inform you, give you the grace; both to know and furthermore, to influence the season ahead, for your benefit and your blessing. You are not a victim you are a victor. God never intended for you to whimper through life reeling from one crisis to the next. For some people, crisis and difficulty have become the parameters of their existence and they hardly recognize or feel comfortable without drama. Your identity is not to be found in your difficulty; your identity is to be found in CHRIST who sits on the throne in your behalf – to bring answers, comfort, and strength in every circumstance.

You are not at the mercy of the whim of the enemy or the capriciousness of a distant God who manipulates your life for some obscure purpose. The Father places no premium on suffering. Jesus suffered so you don't have to: this is the heart of the gospel. God will never put on you, what Jesus died to take off of you. God is not holding out on you; He has no reluctance to move in you and through you, to bring about your victory and success in every endeavor.

You are not a servant to circumstance; you are not a slave to the situation at hand. God made you in His image, to both subdue and have dominion in life, even as He has dominion over the universe (Gen. 1:28).

(Gen. 1:28) And God blessed them, and God said unto

them, "be fruitful, and multiply, and replenish the earth, and subdue it: and have dominion over the fish of the sea, and over the fowl of the air, and over every living thing that moveth upon the earth."

You are a principality and a power. God put you in your life, as He put Adam in the Garden. Satan is the prince of the power of the air because Adam yielded to his temptation, giving Satan the rule over the earth that was originally intended for man. The authority lost in the fall is restored in Christ. You are a tender and keeper of your own life; all of heaven is at your disposal, to put down the interloper and the enemy that would rob you of your blessing. Contrary to unenlightened religious dogma, Satan is not the original prince of the power of the air; nor does he hold those authorities legitimately (Eph. 2:2).

> *(Eph. 2:2) Wherein in time past, ye walked according to the course of this world, according to the prince of the power of the air, the spirit that now worketh in the children of disobedience.*

> *(2 Cor. 10:4) For the weapons of our warfare [are] not carnal, but mighty through God to the pulling down of strong holds.*

God made man a creature of dominion, power, and authority. That which was lost by sin, is restored in Christ (Rom. 5:17). You are not helpless and you are not without resources, to prevail in life.

(Rom. 5:17) For if by one man's offence death reigned by one; much more they, which receive abundance of grace and of the gift of righteousness shall reign in life by one, Jesus Christ.

You must see that you are a principality and power in the earth. The dominion Paul speaks of in the verse above is, first and foremost, executed in the "air realm": This is the realm of principalities, powers, and thrones where angels and demons have commerce, in the unseen, second heaven; that same realm that Jacob saw at Bethel, went he was in flight from the wrath of his brother, Esau (Gen. 28:12).

> *(Gen. 28:12) And he dreamed, and behold a ladder set up on the earth, and the top of it reached to heaven: and behold the angels of God ascending and descending on it.*

There is a natural heaven and a spiritual heaven. Clouds and moisture influence the natural heaven – Angels and Demons influence the spiritual climate. God was impressing upon Jacob, by this vision that his life was not at the whim of natural forces. There is a spiritual firmament of influence and control over life, which will always work in your favor, if you will understand its lessons and cooperate with its initiatives.

Just as there is natural weather in the first heaven (the visible creation), there is spiritual weather affecting your life, in the second heaven. The angels Jacob saw are merely servants and functionaries, tasked to assist mankind as the heirs of salvation in Christ Jesus (Heb. 1:13, 14).

> *(Heb. 1:13-14) But to which of the angels said He, at any time, "Sit on my right hand, until I make thine enemies thy footstool?" 14 Are they not all ministering spirits, sent forth to minister for them who shall be heirs of salvation?*

They (the angels) commiserate in the second heaven as officiators, servants, and functionaries of God, in behalf of you and me, who are kings and priests upon the earth. The second heaven realm, where they serve, is the spiritual realm we rule from: in direct conflict with the enemy who also sits (illegitimately) on thrones and seats of authority, based there. The authority lost in the fall, is restored in Christ (Rom. 5:17-18). It is our job to take our place and rule as principalities and powers, SUBJECT to Christ. This is the rule that Jesus demonstrated in His earth walk.

The sentiments of Whittle's hymn are of value to us beyond their, simple and easy to understand, imagery. There is a science to understanding the weather; as we inquire into the forces of nature that govern the weather, God wants you not only to see His acts, but also to understand His ways (Psalm 103:7).

(Ps. 103:7) He made known his ways unto Moses, his acts unto the children of Israel.

Properly understanding the spiritual lessons and truths behind the natural elements of sky, sea, and earth you can come to the point and the place that you can predict what is on the morrow in your spiritual environment. This is not being a psychic or a clairvoyant.

This is simply sitting at Jesus' feet, learning His ways, and adopting His mind as the template for our own understanding and situation.

In this writing, we will examine the components of nature that comprise our weather and their relationship to biblical metaphors, for the dealings of God. Such metaphors would include: water as a type of the word of God (Eph. 5:26), clouds as representing God's presence and the angels (Rev. 14:15), and lightning striking the ground as a description of Satan's defeat (Luke 10:18).

(Eph. 5:26) That He might sanctify and cleanse it with the washing of water by the word,

(Rev. 14:15) And another angel came out of the temple, crying with a loud voice to him   that sat on the cloud: "Thrust in thy sickle, and reap: for the time is come for thee to reap; for the harvest of the earth is ripe".

(Luke 10:18) And He said unto them, "I beheld Satan as lightning fall from heaven".

Are these metaphors legitimate? It is true any writer can craft an imagery to describe and define a message he wishes to get across. That may have its uses but is it possible that the imagery we draw from scripture can give us a deeper understanding of the ways of God? The Apostle Paul stated in his letter to the Romans that all of creation is actually a template for understanding God, even the very depths of the mysteries of God for those who choose to make the effort to inquire.

(Rom. 1:20) For the invisible things of Him from the creation of the world are clearly seen, being understood by the things that are made, [even] His eternal power and Godhead, so that they are without excuse:

This book will take you on a journey of discovery that will provoke your thinking and inspire your faith. It is presented in an easy to understand format, but you will not be spared the need to use the faculties of your mind. The gospel is for the simple, but it is not for the stupid. Do you know the difference? Stupidity arises out of a refusal to learn. Simplicity is the heart of an inquirer desiring to absorb and learn what God has to say.

There are those who expect bible study to be simple to the point of absurdity. Paul contradicted this thinking by stating in Eph. 3:10 that the wisdom of God is a "manifold wisdom" which means "multi-faceted".

> *(Eph. 3:10) To the intent that now unto the principalities and powers in heavenly [places] might be known by the church the manifold wisdom of God,*

The scriptures contain layers of understanding. This is why Jesus spoke to his disciples over and over again in parables. They came to him eventually inquiring, "why do you speak unto THEM in parables?" (Matt. 13:10). His answer was "because unto you it is given to know …"

> *(Matt. 13:10-12) and the disciples came and said unto him: "Why speakest thou unto them in parables?" 11 He answered and said unto them: "because it is given unto you, to know the mysteries of the kingdom of heaven, but to them it is not given. 12 For whosoever hath, to him shall be given, and he shall have more abundance: but whosoever hath not, from him shall be taken away even that he hath".*

Those who purpose to inquire after deep truth will uncover the things of God, even the deep things of God that are hidden from the unmotivated, casual inquirer. Toward that end, we are going to examine in these pages the scriptural references that are weather-related; and then, look through the lens of the science of meteorology (study of the weather) to find the hidden revelation in nature of God's power and timing. In so doing you will learn key truths to understand the dealings of God both in your personal life and in the world around you. You will be able to position yourself not only to know the spiritual season that you are in, but also to create your own season in God and bring the beneficial rains of God's spirit down in your life for blessing and breakthrough on a daily basis.

Chapter Two: Signs in the Heavens

(Matt. 16:1-3) The Pharisees also with the Sadducees came and tempting him desired that he would shew them a sign from heaven. 2He answered and said unto them: "when it is evening, ye say it will fair weather: for the sky is red. 3And in the morning, it will be foul weather today: for the sky is red and lowring. O ye hypocrites, ye can discern the face of the sky, but can ye not discern the signs of the times?"

Jesus stood before the leaders of His day and rebuked them because of their blindness and inability to discern. God never does anything without first revealing it to His people. He has nothing to hide and nothing to protect. He doesn't need to sneak up on us because there is nothing we could do to abort His will, even if we wished to. Jesus compared the ability to predict weather to the gift of deep discernment. It is available to all who will simply take the time to make the measurement. This verse in Matt. 16:1-3 is the crux of this entire teaching. You have to look deeper into what He is saying and see what He is revealing about Himself. Would Jesus place an expectation on the Pharisees that didn't arise from His own experience? Jesus' own understanding of the nuance of life with His Father, arose from an applied meteorological metaphor. If He expected the rulers in Israel to discern the spiritual climate around them, under the limitations of the Old Covenant, and in their own lost condition, it only indicates that this is how Jesus Himself looked at the world around Him. He discerned its spiritual climate with a view to understanding what lie ahead. Jesus was the master of the winds and the waves. He spoke to storms and stilled their fury. If our Savior commanded the natural elements of the first heaven, it then follows that He likewise commanded the second heaven. Demons feared Him. Angels served Him. He could walk into a city, know its principalities and powers, and command their fear and respect. He stood on the brow of a hill overlooking Jerusalem and read the spiritual climate of the city. He knew they would reject Him and crucify Him.

> *(Matt. 23:37) O Jerusalem, Jerusalem, [thou] that killest the prophets, and stonest them which are sent unto thee, how often would I have gathered thy children together, even as a hen gathereth her chickens under [her] wings, and ye would not!*

We are exhorted to let the mind of Christ be in us. Along with the Christ mentality, comes the ability to discern as He did, know as He did, and command as He did. You have more authority than you know. You have more access to gifts of discernment than you know. The most spiritual among us, have only just begun to plumb the depths of knowledge, authority, and dominion that is available to us, as believers. As we gain, learn, and understand then, our works would become the greater works; even greater than

Jesus did in the earth, as He predicted. As you discern the ecosystem of the Spirit of God whirling on the inside of you, then you will effortlessly look around you and identify, with transparency, every ploy and assault of the enemy. You must discern yourself before you can discern the enemy and his tactics.

So we see Jesus reproved the spiritual leaders of his day for knowing how to predict the weather, yet possessing no understanding of the Kingdom of God. Notice in Matt. 16:1-3 they wanted a "sign from heaven". What they didn't understand, was that the sign wouldn't come from heaven – rather the HEAVENS THEMSELVES WERE the sign. God created the weather that controls the earth's climate, not only to nourish the earth, but also to say something to us about God's immutable purposes; how we can anticipate and cooperate with His personal plan for our lives, as well as His larger purposes.

> *(Ps. 19:1) To the chief Musician, A Psalm of David. The heavens declare the glory of God and the firmament sheweth his handiwork.*

The heavens declare the glory of God. This is what Rom. 1:20 refers. The invisible things of God are known in the visible creation. In this case, the weather system that governs the earth, reveals to you truth and understanding of the unseen spiritual environment that constitutes the second heaven (where angels and demons come into conflict and affect the affairs of men and the affairs of your personal life). The heavens declare the glory of God. What is the glory of God? Philippians 4:19 tells us that the glory of God is where our supply is found:

(Phil .4:19) But my God shall supply all your need according to his riches in glory by Christ Jesus.

Whatever the glory is, it contains in embryo, the inventory of everything you could ever ask the Father. The glory is not just a cosmic or celestial decoration intended to reveal God's fashion sense. The glory is potent and practical and has bearing on our lives! If the glory is where our riches in Christ are found, and the resource from which all our needs are met, then we better find out where this glory is! Paul knew the secret of this mystery but rather than hiding it away behind some mystical code, he declared it openly:

(Col. 1:27) To whom God would make known what [is] the riches of the glory of this mystery among the Gentiles; which is Christ in you, the hope of glory.

So what is the glory? It is the resource from which every answer to prayer originates. Where is the glory? Whatever the glory is and whatever its function, it is IN US. Therefore, when the Psalmist says that the "HEAVENS DECLARE THE GLORY OF GOD", we take that to mean that the heavens declare the power, resource, and reality of processes originating in God, and at work in and through us! So, everything we touch on in this book is not some unreachable something, only available to the elite mystics. It is accessible to every born again boy, girl, man, and woman that will take the time and care to seek out these truths in the scripture, and look around them to learn what is their birthright and dominion in the earth.

Jesus warned his followers about sign seekers. A sign seeker looks for something arising from superstition. As a believer, you are gifted by God to look past the natural and reveal the mysteries of God. The basic nature of the ancient sign seekers was very much, the same as those today who seek out clairvoyants and psychics. They want something supernatural in their life, which doesn't require faith on their part, to align with and reap the benefits. The Apostle Paul talked about two classes of inquirers into spiritual things. He distinguished them as either "sign seekers" or "wisdom seekers".

> *(1Cor. 1:22) For the Jews require a sign and the Greeks seek after wisdom.*

Sign seekers are those looking for something external to themselves, through which, God will independently indicate to them, what His divine will is. Wisdom seekers are intellectual empiricists for whom all things must "add up" and pass the muster of their rational thinking process. Both sign seekers and wisdom seekers are cut out of the same cloth. They depend on these senses, and their own rationalizations and analytical frames of reference to quantify the things they value. They forget that God's ways are not our ways; although He intends that we know His ways, nonetheless. God is not a God of logic. Neither will He be confined to the subjectivism of the mystical or tabloid spiritual experience and goose bumps. You must come to Him and sit at His feet on His terms and His timetable. Logic, rationale, and emotionalism must wait at the door while you commune and sup with Him, allowing Him to set the agenda and teach you, by the means of methods of His choosing.

> *(Ps. 103:7) He made known his ways unto Moses, His acts unto the children of Israel.*

God's ways are knowable: God's ways are knowable for

those open minded enough to set aside the demands of superstition, on the one hand, and the tyrannical demands of pragmatism, on the other. The ways of God do not register upon the rationale expectation of wisdom seekers, or upon the religious sensibilities of the sign seekers. God's ways are available for us to learn through the instrumentality of human intuition. God created and provided this for us, in order to make the revelational leap across the gap of human credibility, and access the stream of His thoughts directly, whether we understand the experience or not.

The Jews confronting Jesus, (in Matt. 16:1-3) wanted a sign in the heavens – an actual meteorological event that was beyond the norm to such a degree, that it would confirm Jesus' identity as the Messiah, without actually requiring faith on their part. In other words, it wouldn't have been good enough for Jesus to say: "Ok, here is your sign; tomorrow the sky will be blue. That will prove My Messianic claims." They would have scoffed at this, as they were expecting something out of the ordinary and unusual. Furthermore, they wanted this sign to be from heaven because, in their thinking, anything that happened in heaven was beyond the ability of any man to do by trickery or fraud. In saying this, they betrayed their thinking about what comprised spiritual validity, from their view of God. If you are going to sit at the Master's feet, you must lose the attitude and the demand that you set the bar of validity on that which He shows you, or the means that He employs to teach you. He is God, He knows more, and He's bigger than you are. You must come to Him on His terms because He is the ultimate "A" type personality.

As the ancient philosophers and sign seekers, so people are the same today. For all our modernity and advanced technology, man only believes what he sees and accepts what he can measure. The sense knowledge realm of the scientist and the superstitious can be manipulated. We must look deeper. Our common understanding of God is to expect Him to act completely independent of human instrumentality. The problem with this, is that God will SELDOM do ANYTHING independent of cooperation with, and in concert, with man. Even in sending Jesus, it was necessary for Mary to say: "Be it unto me even as you have said…" (See Luke 1:38). God's purposes are worked out in concert with man, and with man's cooperation. This is why the prophetic is available in the earth so you can intimately know God's plans and purposes in your life, not just so you are aware of what God will independently do, quite the contrary. The prophetic is there in concert with the voice of God, to reveal to you what God will ONLY do with your cooperation and alignment to His divine will revealed and confirmed in your life.

Jesus' response to this challenge was to question the definition his accusers held, in terms of what constitutes an unimpeachable testimony of the hand of God at work or the validation of the man or woman that God might choose. In our own day many times what we describe as a validated testimony, is simply asking God to move in such an independent and evidentiary way, that it doesn't even require faith to believe what it happening. A common example would be the prophetic word. When a prophecy comes forth, many people reject what God is saying unless it reveals something to, or through, the prophet that he or she couldn't have possibly known. This is the word of knowledge component in the prophetic. The word of knowledge is for the UNBELIEVER, not the BELIEVER. Are you a believer? Then grow up and learn how to hear from God without the spiritual parlor trick of a word of knowledge, to circumvent the requirement of faith on your part. Let us remember if we call ourselves BELIEVERS, that the word of knowledge component of a prophetic word (according to Paul) is for the UNBELIEVER, not for the believer (see 1 Cor. 14:24-25).

> *(1Cor. 14:24-25) But if all prophesy, and there come in one that believeth not, or [one] unlearned, he is convinced of all, he is judged of all: 25And thus are the secrets of his heart made manifest; and so falling down on [his] face he will worship God, and report that God is in you of a truth.*

As a believer, you must get past expecting God, every time He speaks to you, to satisfy your capacity for unbelief, or you won't accept what is said. Entrenched unbelief only yields to empirical measurement or superstitious mysticism. Both can lead you down the primrose path to deception. It is time to grow up and to learn God's ways, as well as His acts. As a believer, you are called and intended by God, to be an ACTIVE INITIATOR of His purpose and not merely a PASSIVE RECIPIENT of His process. You need to make a positive choice in your life, not to be a sign seeker like these Pharisees in Matthew 16:1-3. It is unbelief to seek an independent sign; we are not to be sign seekers. Those who follow fleeces, get fleeced! You must grow in your spiritual sensibilities so, as Jesus, you can measure (by God's perceptive sense on the inside of you) and know exactly what today holds, and what tomorrow brings. You may not have every detail, but you won't be caught unawares. We don't follow signs, but God intends that SIGNS TO FOLLOW US.

(Mar 16:17) And these signs shall follow them that believe; in My name shall they cast out devils; they shall speak with new tongues;

God doesn't want you following signs, but He did say that signs would follow you, as a believer. God poured out His Spirit without measure, upon Jesus. The measurelessness of the Spirit of God is available to you and me today because Jesus said He would take of the Father's and give it unto us. The day is coming that, just as believers speak in tongues at will: they shall prophesy at will, heal at will, and perform miracles at will, just as Jesus did. Do you see the difference? Signs following are the hallmark of a mature believer. Sign seekers never get past the infancy of unbelief. Believers who mature past sign seeking will become intrinsically involved in the atmosphere that initiates signs, miracles and wonders where they have not been in evidence. At this level of maturity, you are the ACTIVE INITIATOR of the miraculous and not just a consumer or observer of the miraculous.

Jesus struggled with sign-seeking and rationalistic demands in his own disciples. They despised the practice of speaking in parables. They wanted naked truth. They wanted instant results. Even when He stood before them in resurrected form, Thomas wanted a SIGN and unimpeachable evidence that He was risen. Jesus gave Thomas what he asked for with the gentle rebuke

(John 20:29) Jesus saith unto him:" Thomas, because thou hast seen me, thou hast believed: blessed [are] they that have not seen, and [yet] have believed".

The Prophet Isaiah speaking prophetically as the Messiah,

not only pointed to Jesus as the sign, but to the people of God, as symbols (in them) of God's authority and majesty in the earth.

> *(Isa. 8:18) Behold, I and the children whom the LORD hath given me [are] for signs and for wonders in Israel from the LORD of hosts, which dwelleth in mount Zion.*

In that context, you can now know that God doesn't want you to SEEK a sign; He wants you (as Jesus is) to be a SIGN (within yourself) of the power and glory of God in the earth. When you make that transition, then you are eligible to mature into what Paul called: "the full measure and stature of Christ on the earth" (Eph. 4:11-18). Jesus didn't pray for the weather – He CONTROLLED the weather. We are not speaking just of natural elements, (though we don't exclude them) but we are also talking about the spiritual climate of your own life. As Jesus controlled the winds, waves, the clouds, and lightning; even so are you authorized and empowered, IN CHRIST, to set your own season with God and bring the beneficial rains of the Spirit of God down upon the geography of your own life.

It is the hallmark of a Pharisee to require something other than the testimony of God's word to overcome doubt and unbelief. Experiences, miracles, signs, and wonders are fleeting experiences that will elude you, when you need their testimony most desperately in your life. God's word stands forever. When God's word is established in your heart, you are not merely a consumer of the miraculous, you are a producer of the miraculous; participating with God, Himself, in effecting your own deliverance and the divine intervention of His grace in the lives of others. This book will show you how by revelatory understanding to identify what God is doing in the earth and your life; to cooperate with that process; and further, to become an initiator and steward of the Lordship of Christ, flowing out of your faith to transform your own experience and the experience of others, regarding the kingdom of God as a resource for blessing and breakthrough.

CHAPTER THREE: DISCERN YOUR SEASON

God created the earth to reflect his truth and glory. Study of the weather (learning to discern the face of the sky), will bring understanding and insight into the Kingdom of God in your life.

> *(Psa 19:1) To the chief Musician, A Psalm of David: The heavens declare the glory of God and the firmament sheweth his handiwork. "*

Col.1:27 tells us that the message Paul preached was one of "Christ in you the Hope of Glory". If the heavens declare the glory of God, they are, therefore, declaring something that is on the inside of you. They are speaking of "Christ in you, the hope of Glory". The sky, the weather system, the climate that churns in our atmosphere is echoing, foreshadowing, and demonstrating the fact that, on the inside of you, is a spiritual climate that can and will, benefit your life spiritually (just as the natural climate benefits the earth).This is more than just a theological understanding of God, Savior, and Creator.

The kingdom of God is the "basilea" of God--meaning the "divine rule or sphere of authority".

> *KINGDOM: [Greek: Basilea] the territory that is subject to the rule of a king, royal power, kingship, dominion, rule; not to be confused with an actual kingdom, but rather the right (or authority) to rule over a kingdom of the royal power of Jesus (as the triumphant Messiah), and the dignity conferred on Christians in the Messiah's kingdom (as used in the New Testament.to refer to the reign of the Messiah).*

God created man to rule the earth, not be ruled by it, or by any other spiritual being other than Himself. He gave man authority to subdue and to have dominion. You are a creature of dominion. You are destined to subdue the environment you find yourself in. You are not a victim. You are a victor. God put you in your life like He put Adam and Eve in the garden – to subdue and have dominion over it.

> *(Gen 1:28) And God blessed them, and God said unto them: "be fruitful, and multiply, and replenish the earth, and subdue it, and have dominion..."*

He positioned Himself in creation to make His power available to us through faith and expectation. Ruling and reigning is not possible outside of Christ. We rule and reign in Him, and through dependence upon the Spirit of God on the inside of us. It is, therefore, important, that we have more than a rudimentary understanding of the Spirit of

God. The Spirit of God (the Holy Ghost) can be known and understood. His very nature is that of a helper, teacher, and comforter. In these roles, He is more than just one thing to us. Isaiah 11:2 tells us there are seven spirits of God that you can call on by adopting the posture toward God that your circumstance calls for. Sometimes, it is a posture of confronting the powers of darkness. Other times, it is a posture of worship or adoration--but ALWAYS a posture of prayer. Prayer provokes heaven to rain down upon you. Prayer creates the condition of humility (by which you "GO LOW" to generate a "low pressure system") that the seven Spirits of God will bend low, to pour out the beneficial rains of God's blessing upon you.

> *(Isa 11:2) And the spirit of the LORD shall rest upon him, the spirit of wisdom and understanding, the spirit of counsel and might, the spirit of knowledge and of the fear of the LORD.*

Just as there are seven spirits of God, there are likewise seven jet streams that govern the natural weather systems of the earth. There is a current to the Spirit of God. The very word in the Old Testament for Spirit is "Ruach", which means a blast or current of air or wind. God's Spirit in your life is dynamic and directional. Those who say God never directs you or speaks directionally to you, are completely incorrect. God's Spirit is that of multiple currents, rivers, and winds that are constantly coming to bear on your life. As you come to cooperate and identify these currents, you can position yourself for blessing and benefit ON PURPOSE, not just sit around wondering when God is going to bless you.

The heavens declare the glory of God. They declare something of what God's glory is and how it works on the inside of us. You have an ecosystem and a spiritual climate of God's making on the inside of you. This can be understood, provoked to your blessing, and cooperated with, for your benefit. This is God's handiwork, revealing something of Himself to us, (for our own benefit) in our interaction with His realm – the realm of the Spirit – the seven-fold Spirit of God. The natural jet streams bend and move, tracking and pouring themselves into "low-pressure systems". When you "go low" (choosing the posture of humility), the seven Spirits of God bend low into the spiritual climate of your life, bringing the beneficial rains of His blessing. In other words, by understanding humility as a weapon of spiritual warfare, you can set your own season in God, drive off the enemy, and cause the dry and barren experiences of life to blossom and bloom, under the beneficial rains of the Spirit of God. All this occurs, by adopting humility and "going low" to attract the seven spirits of God, to find you and establish over you a beneficial ecosystem of growth and blessing.

(Jas. 4:6) But He giveth more grace. Wherefore he saith:
"God resisteth the proud, but giveth grace unto the humble."

The kingdom of God is reflective of God's character. We need and want the kingdom to show up in our day. Whatever the kingdom is, we have to remember that Jesus stressed that it is not outward but inward, first and foremost. Humility on your part brings the kingdom online and makes it active in your behalf. God has an autonomic response to humility– just like a jet stream has an automatic response of moving toward and pouring out its rains and moisture on the nearest low-pressure system to it. What do you and I need to know about the kingdom of God, to see it manifest in our lives? Just what is the kingdom of God?

> *(Matt. 5:3) Blessed [are] the poor in spirit: for theirs is the kingdom of heaven.*

To begin to understand the kingdom, you must first know where it is and where it isn't. The kingdom of God or the Kingdom of Heaven (the two terms are held as synonymous for the purpose of this writing) isn't a planet somewhere or some science fiction dimension. Some, do in fact, believe that the kingdom of God is a planet or a realm in space. There are those that believe that heaven and the throne of God, are located in the vast reaches of space beyond the northern sky. When you understand some things about God and about His eternal nature, you will know this cannot be true (anymore than, hell is located in the depths of the earth under your feet). Einstein proved that time and space (three-dimensional space) are intrinsically connected to one another. In other words, any given place in the universe or natural creation, is bound in time and, therefore, temporal in nature.

Paul said this, himself, in 2 Corinthians:

> *(2Cor. 4:18) While we look not at the things which are seen, but at the things which are not seen: for the things which are seen [are] temporal; but the things which are not seen [are] eternal.*

This verse proves that heaven and the throne of God are located nowhere in the natural universe. The things that you can see are "temporal" (temporary), subject to decay. God is eternal; He exists outside of time and space. He can experience the end from the beginning, just as you can hold this book up and open the covers, to see the end and beginning, simultaneously. So, while the kingdom exists, it is not geo-located in a manner that you and I could get in a spacecraft and navigate ourselves to its location. So if Matt. 6:33 tells us we should be seeking the kingdom, whence do we turn?

> *(Matt. 6:33) But seek ye first the kingdom of God, and his righteousness; and all these things shall be added unto you.*

Jesus made it quite plain when He taught (and Paul later affirmed) that whatever the kingdom is, and wherever it is, it originates IN YOU (Luke 17:21). The kingdom that is not IN YOU is not the kingdom. The Jesus that doesn't dwell in your heart by faith, is not the one that bled and died on your behalf. In turning to Jesus, we are turning within to find the Lamb (slain at the foundation of the world), sitting on the throne of our hearts.

Jesus always spoke very plainly about the kingdom. He was demanded to explain when the kingdom would be restored to Israel. His answer seemed to be changing the subject, but in reality it wasn't. Those interrogating Him were asking Him to explain God's linear purpose through time, with respect to, the fortunes of the nation of Israel. He basically points out (in Luke 17: 20, 21), that they were asking the wrong question.

 You will never get a right answer until you ask the right question. Jesus turns the entire discussion into something relevant to men and woman of God, in all ages and at every level of experience.

> *(Luke 17:20-21) and when He was demanded of the Pharisees, when the kingdom of God should come, He*

answered them and said: "The kingdom of God cometh not with observation: 21 neither shall they say, 'Lo here! Or, lo there!' For, behold, the kingdom of God is within you."

Whatever the kingdom is, it is on the inside of you. The kingdom of God is a spiritual environment (or ecosystem) that originates, or finds its fountainhead or origin, within you. Sense knowledge minds will never comprehend this. Religious mentalities cannot fathom this. They are always looking beyond that which is accessible, because their "god" is not a God who is near but rather a far-off god. Our God is not a far-off God. He is as close to us as our hands and feet – yes, even as close as the breath of our nostrils.

This is the mystery of Godliness. The concept of the kingdom as something external to you is misdirecting, if you accept what Jesus told the Pharisees. They (no doubt) rejected His statement as vain spiritualizing, of a very practical question. We must accept, and realize that, the natural weather system above us declares the glory of God and the kingdom of God. So, in coming to an understanding of the true and spiritual heavens around us, you are coming to know your own personal spiritual environment (INSIDE YOU): one that can be influenced, shaped, and directed to your benefit and blessing, in God's purposes for your life. If you can discern the climate of God on the inside of your own human spirit, you can accurately expect and anticipate what is taking place, not only in your now, but in the coming days as well. In fact, you can not only discern the immediate spiritual forecast of blessing or calamity ahead for you, you can actually set your own season in God.

Much of this process (of setting your own season) relies on

the words of your mouth and the condition of your heart before God. This is what Jesus was referring to when He said: "out of the abundance of the heart the mouth speaks; make the tree good and its fruit good, or make the tree evil and its fruit evil".

> *(Matt. 12:33) Either make the tree good, and his fruit good or else make the tree corrupt, and his fruit corrupt: for the tree is known by [his] fruit*

What is the fruit of your heart? The fruit of your heart is, what the words of your mouth produce in your life. "Life and death are in the power of the tongue." Life and death are the fruits of the tongue – originating in either a corrupt natural mind, or a mind that has put on the mind, or mentality, of Christ.

> *(Prov. 18:21) Death and life [are] in the power of the tongue: and they that love it shall eat the fruit thereof.*

Both conservative Christianity and liberal Christianity, obstinately reject this thinking, though it is the clear testimony of scripture. James said that the tongue is the most unruly evil.

> *(James 3:8) But the tongue can no man tame; it is an unruly evil, full of deadly poison.*

If for one moment, we accepted the truth of what the Word itself says about the tongue, we would become forever accountable; for our words, our thoughts, and our attitudes are the source of much suffering and struggle that we face. We would much rather adopt a dark and troubling picture, of a sovereign God capriciously bringing calamity into our lives, through no fault or involvement of our own. Is this what the scripture teaches? A precursory examination, of passages dealing with the power of the tongue, will always put the onus directly upon us not, some capricious act of an austere God regarding much of human suffering and struggle. This is our accountability, but it is also our ray of hope. God has made it possible for us (through prayer, declaration, and profession) to influence the character of the days ahead for us all through the power of our words.

The indulgence of your words are predictors of your future. Negative words release creative power to produce negative circumstances. This negativity originates in your human spirit and influences your outward life; if you believe what the scriptures say, you cannot deny the truth of this.

> *(Matt. 7:17-18) Even so every good tree bringeth forth good fruit; but a corrupt tree bringeth forth evil fruit. 18 A good tree cannot bring forth evil fruit, neither [can] a corrupt tree bring forth good fruit.*

If you don't like what is in your life, then change what is in your heart. If you change what is in your heart, your circumstances of life will adjust to that inward reality, by the creative power of the words that proceed out of your mouth.

> *(Prov. 15:4) A wholesome tongue [is] a tree of life: but perverseness therein [is] a breach in the spirit.*

Therefore, we see that the inner climate of your human spirit (for good or for evil) serves as the preamble and the predictor for the immediate circumstances, that are about to unfold in your life. If you choose to understand this, and align yourself with these realities, you will begin to be a person who sets their own season in life. You will know what is on the morrow and by repentance and discernment, evade many of the trials and troubles ahead by your humility, your heartfelt prayers, and bold professions of faith.

In the Old Testament, there are found among King David's mighty men, those who were "men of understanding concerning the times". Drawing closer to the return of Christ, understanding the times becomes more important for the believer.

> *(1Chron. 12:32) And of the children of Issachar, [which were men] that had understanding of the times, to know what Israel ought to do; the heads of them [were] two hundred; and all their brethren [were] at their commandment.*

If the inhabitants of Jerusalem had understanding of their times, they might have hesitated before crucifying the Lord of Glory. Many years ago, the Holy Spirit spoke to me concerning Matt. 16:1 that, through studying his handiwork in the weather, insight may be gained pertaining to the kingdom. The heavens, when you study them, will declare to you the glory of God. The natural creation will cause you to understand His eternal power and Godhood. You can read creation as infallibly as you can read the bible – perhaps, more so at times. You will know the day of your visitation. You will know that season that God is prepared to move in your life, to bring you into your destined promise. You will know, and will cooperate with, God's plan; instead of inadvertently resisting the Holy Spirit, as the city of Jerusalem did.

(Luke 19:43-44) For the days shall come upon thee, that thine enemies shall cast a trench about thee, and compass thee round, and keep thee in on every side, 44And shall lay thee even with the ground, and thy children within thee; and they shall not leave in thee one stone upon another; because thou knewest not the time of thy visitation.

By studying the creation, you learn of the Creator. The study of nature confirms the timeless truths of the Word of God…again and again. In years gone by, many great scientists and naturalists held this conviction. Men such as Audubon, and even Einstein who observed, "God didn't play dice with the universe." Paul the Apostle taught that God, as Creator, is made known through the creation.

(Rom. 1:20) For the invisible things of him from the creation of the world are clearly seen, being understood by the things that are made, [even] His eternal power and Godhead; so that they are without excuse.

So, in studying these things and making the connection between natural weather phenomena and the things of God, we are not exercising vain imagination; but on the contrary, we're discovering the ancient and hidden truths that have been available for centuries to those discerning enough and desirous enough to know God beyond the casual observations and measurements of dead religion. There is much to be gleaned through observation of the handiwork of God in comparison with the truths of the gospel. In this writing, the earth's atmosphere and its composite elements represent different aspects of the nature of God, the character of man, and the spiritual dimension that governs humanity. Let us consider these elements:

PNEUMA: The New Testament word for "spirit" such as the Spirit of God is pneuma. The term for natural wind and the Spirit of God are one and the same.

> *(1 John 4:2) Hereby, know ye the Spirit [Greek word Pneuma] of God: Every spirit that confesseth that Jesus Christ is come in the flesh is of God:*

SPIRIT: pneuma - a movement of air (a gentle blast); of the wind, hence the wind itself; breath of nostrils or mouth.

EARTH: Jesus himself taught in the parable of the sower that the earth represents the heart of man.

> *(Matt. 13:19) When any one heareth the word of the kingdom, and understandeth [it] not, then cometh the wicked [one], and catcheth away that which was sown in his heart. This is he which received seed by the way side.*

The sea and its tides are representative of the wicked; for Isaiah said "the wicked are as the raging sea…" Men are likewise spoken of as trees, plants, rocks, clouds, rivers, etc. All the things that make up our natural earth, when studied as a SPIRITUAL environment, will cause you to understand some deep things of God – unknown and indiscernible to the casual observer.

> *(Isa. 57:20) But the wicked [are] like the troubled sea, when it cannot rest, whose waters cast up mire and dirt.*

Upon first researching this subject, there were no great flashes of revelation that came to me. After weeks of research, I gained nothing that I felt was God breathed or

God revealed. I set all the research aside and began to pray. One morning, insight came. Upon waking, a simple question presented itself to my thoughts: "How many jet streams are there?" Again, jet streams are powerful wind currents that circle the globe in the upper atmosphere. They govern the distribution of clouds and moisture in the earth's many climates. When the question was posed to me by the Spirit of God, I immediately knew what He was referring: There are, in fact, seven jet streams or great tunnels of wind that circle the globe. The Bible word for "Spirit" is a "blast of air..." John the Revelator spoke, four different times, of the "Seven Spirits or Sevenfold Spirit of God..."

(Rev. 1:4) John to the seven churches which are in Asia: Grace [be] unto you, and peace, from Him which is, and which was, and which is to come; and from the seven Spirits which are before His throne.

(Rev. 3:1) And unto the angel of the church in Sardis write: These things saith He that hath the seven Spirits of God, and the seven stars; I know thy works, that thou hast a name that thou livest, and art dead.

(Rev. 4:5) And out of the throne proceeded lightnings and thunderings and voices: and [there were] seven lamps of fire burning before the throne, which are the seven Spirits of God.

(Rev 5:6) And I beheld, and, lo, in the midst of the throne and of the four beasts, and in the midst of the elders, stood a Lamb as it had been slain, having seven horns and seven eyes, which the seven Spirits of God are sent forth into all the earth.

The word "spirit" in each of these cases is "pneuma" or "wind". I saw, at that moment, that the seven jet streams had been created by God to reflect His governing influence over the earth. These seven jet streams are analogous the Seven Spirits of God. From that point, I returned to my study finding analogies and types that reflect spiritual truths in many aspects of the earth's weather system. The interaction of sun, sea, and earth with the atmosphere became (for me) a shadow of God's interaction with man and man's involvement in the dimension of spiritual things.

God spoke, through the prophet, that He would do nothing on the earth before He first revealed His plan to His people. A meteorologist can look at natural weather and predict future conditions. Likewise, a child of God can look at the spiritual condition of the generation he lives in, and predict the future of that generation. This is not based on super-spiritual guesswork, but on the precedents found in the scriptures and revealed by the Spirit. Throughout the scriptures, the things of God are taught in meteorological terms. This writing attempts to be a comprehensive treatment of that subject, as a whole, with a view to bringing understand and light to the reader, concerning his personal condition before God.

CHAPTER FOUR: SET YOUR SEASON IN GOD

Jesus, in Matthew's gospel, dropped a clue to a great mystery in creation, through which, the nature and glory of God would be revealed.

> *(Matt. 16:1-3) The Pharisees also with the Sadducees came, and tempting. desired Him that He would shew them a sign from heaven. 2He answered and said unto them: "when it is evening, ye say, [It will be] fair weather: for the sky is red. 3And in the morning, [It will be] foul weather today: for the sky is red and lowring. O [ye] hypocrites, ye can discern the face of the sky; but can ye not [discern] the signs of the times?"*

Here is the challenge to the Pharisees: "You can tell the weather, but you don't understand the kingdom?" The inference is, that the weather and the Kingdom have something in common. If you study the weather, (i.e. meteorology) you will acquire knowledge about the kingdom. As we have established from Luke 17:20, 21, "the kingdom is within you". Therefore, in becoming acquainted with the weather, you learn of the kingdom; in which case, you are learning about God and His principles at work in your life. This is not just a convenient teaching tool on Jesus' part. This analogy is not by mistake, mind you, but rather God created the forces that make up our global climate. He did this in such a way, as upon study, to reflect and reveal His nature and principles of His Kingdom.

The word weather is defined as, "the state of the atmosphere with respect to wind, temperature, cloudiness, moisture, pressure, etc." Now, think about weather-related terms we use to describe our frame of mind. We might say we are: "under the weather; or "on the sunny side of life", etc...

Jesus spoke, as well, of building men's lives in preparation for life's storms (another meteorological reference). If you understood HOW the storms come, then you would be better prepared, even as natural preparedness saves lives.

> *(Matt. 16:1-3) The Pharisees also with the Sadducees came, and tempting desired Him that He would shew them a sign from heaven. 2He answered and said unto them: "when it is evening, ye say, [It will be] fair weather: for the sky is red. 3And in the morning, [It will be] foul weather today: for the sky is red and lowring. O [ye] hypocrites, ye can discern the face of the sky; but can ye not [discern] the signs of the times?"*

Man's interest in the weather reflects the profound effect it has on all aspects of our lives. Some studies show, that even in a natural sense, the weather actually affects the way we feel both emotionally and physically. Areas of low pressure may cause a period of low feelings for some people. There is a form of depression called S.A.D. (Seasonal Affective Disorder) that affects some people only in winter, when they receive less sunlight.

Jesus also taught extensively concerning the Kingdom of God in agricultural terms. Obviously, agriculture is weather dependent. Agrarian terminology fits easily within the vernacular of Christianity. The average Christian's vocabulary, in regard to his spiritual condition, is replete with meteorological references. "I'm going through a dry place," one may say, or "you are facing a real storm in this circumstance..." Times of refreshing are often described as rain or "showers of blessing." Paul spoke to Timothy of spiritual "seasons" that he would experience, as a young apostle.

> *(2 Tim. 4:2) Preach the word; be instant in season, out of season; reprove, rebuke, exhort with all longsuffering and doctrine.*

Webster defines the word season as: "a period associated with some phase or activity of agriculture (as growth or harvesting), characterized by a particular kind of weather."

The scriptures consistently use meteorological references speaking of the church or the individual believer (wheat, trees, vines, etc.). The basic attributes of the Christ-like personality are termed "fruits of the spirit."

(Gal 5:22-23) But the fruit of the Spirit is love, joy, peace, longsuffering, gentleness, goodness, faith, 23Meekness, temperance: against such there is no law.

What can we learn from this? Fruits do not grow year round, they are seasonal. Then, the characteristics of Christ, as they manifest in your life on a basis analogous to fruit are, therefore, LIKEWISE SEASONAL. You won't feel loving, joyful, or peaceful ALL THE TIME. This is natural, and to be expected. Various fruits have different growing seasons. Understanding the forces that control these seasons, and their respective analogies in the scriptures, affords deep insight into the ebb and flow of life in Christ Jesus.

There are many varied factors that contribute to the weather we experience. Science teaches that a series of interactions between earth and its atmosphere lead to the weather we know today. All of the following contribute to the shaping of the earth's climate: the combination of volcanic activity, earthquakes and plate tectonics, the oceans, the atmosphere, and the influence of the earth's magnetic field, and also radiation from the sun.

Just as there are varied factors that contribute to natural weather, likewise, there are many elements that influence the spiritual climate of your life. To understand these influences, is to better understand yourself and your relationship to the things of God. The often asked question "Why?" is addressed in this analogy as a many-faceted issue. You are not walking through life as one of God's clay pigeons with a target on your back, for Him to hurl lightning bolts of sovereignty into your circumstances. Studying the analogy of weather, compared to the spiritual condition, reveals many contributing forces behind the events and circumstances in your life that you can, in fact, INFLUENCE and ANTICIPATE. You can FORECAST your spiritual season and INFLUENCE what comes next for your benefit and the benefit of others. Most importantly to understand, is the degree to which your decisions strengthen or weaken the probability of immediate blessing of God outpouring in your life.

The earth influences the weather and represents man's self-determination before God. Influencing the weather through magnetic fields, volcanoes, etc.: the earth is representative of man because, God made man out of the dust of the earth.

> *(Gen 2:7) And the LORD God formed man [of] the dust of the ground, and breathed into his nostrils the breath of life, and man became a living soul.*

Jesus said that the heart is like soil or earth. There is an earth within you whose disposition has a direct bearing on the spiritual influence that will shape the immediate events about to play out in your life.

> *(Luke 8:11-12) Now, the parable is this: The seed is the word of God. 12Those by the way side are they that hear; then cometh the devil, and taketh away the word out of their hearts, lest they should believe and be saved.*

As a human being, your choices, decisions, and general posture towards God, profoundly affect the quality of your life. It is either a downward or upward curve, in whatever given situation you may be facing at the present time. God is not arbitrarily damning one and sparing another. At some level, your actions and attitudes determine the outcome of your life generally, and your circumstances specifically.

Air is an essential component of weather and represents the Spirit of God. The word "spirit" in the New Testament is "Pneuma", meaning literally "a blast or current of air hence the wind itself" The apostle, John stated that Jesus declared "God is a Spirit, and that true worshippers would worship in truth and in spirit".

> *(John 4:24) God [is] a Spirit: and they that worship him must worship [Him] in spirit and in truth.*

In this description is seen (as previously mentioned) the analogy of the nature of God with the winds that govern the earth's weather, which are called "jet streams." John, the Revelator, also spoke of the Sevenfold Spirit of God. This is not a mistake or coincidence. God has so ordered His creation to "declare his glory" to those who will take time to study it, in conjunction with the scriptures.

> *(Rev. 1:4) John to the seven churches which are in Asia: Grace [be] unto you, and peace, from Him which is, and which was, and which is to come; and from the seven Spirits which are before His throne.*

> *(Ps. 19:1) To the chief Musician, A Psalm of David. The heavens declare the glory of God; and the firmament sheweth his handiwork.*

Consider the weather and the earth's magnetism: It is known that the earth's magnetic field also affects climates around the world. Magnetic north is the point that helps you find your way with a compass. It has been noted that there are slight changes as the earth's magnetism moves slightly every year. Sometimes, the earth's magnetism is thought to have shifted dramatically, flipping from the Northern Hemisphere to the Southern Hemisphere.

The scriptures often refer to geographical locations and points on the compass as illustrations of God's nature and his dealings with man. The city of God, according to the Psalmist, is to be found in the north. Lucifer conceived rebellion in his heart, seeking to sit "on the sides of the north."

> *(Ps. 48: 2) Beautiful for situation, the joy of the whole earth, [is] mount Zion, [on] the sides of the north, the city of the great King.*

> *(Isa. 14:12-13) How art thou fallen from heaven, O Lucifer, son of the morning [how] art thou cut down to the ground, which didst weaken the nations! 13For thou hast said in thine heart, I will ascend into heaven: I will exalt my throne above the stars of God: I will sit also upon the mount of the congregation, in the sides of the north:"*

Now it is implausible to assume that God is speaking literally regarding the location of his judgment bar. If that would be so, then Eskimos in the Yukon would be closer to God than Australian Aborigines, just by virtue of their homeland. If then, God is not speaking literally, then "the North" has a figurative meaning. This figurative application of north, south, east, and west bears directly on the comparison of spiritual things with the weather because, the primary difference between north and south the magnetism by which we calibrate our compasses. The magnetic field on the earth represents the drawing power of God's Spirit.

(John 6:44) No man can come to me, except the Father which hath sent me draw him: and I will raise him up at the last day.

(Song of Sol. 1:4) Draw me, we will run after thee: the king hath brought me into his chambers: we will be glad and rejoice in thee, we will remember thy love more than wine: the upright love thee.

(Hos. 11:4) I drew them with cords of a man, with bands of love: and I was to them as they that take off the yoke on their jaws, and I laid meat unto them.

North represents judgment, while south symbolizes blessing: The prophet Habakkuk wrote that God "comes from Teman," meaning "south." Now what can be deduced from these statements? God is omnipresent so, He cannot be in one place and not be in another. Therefore, to say "He sits in judgment on the sides of the north" or, that "He came from Teman" is not telling you to hang a left at Greenland to catch Him at His judgment bar, and take a right at Australia to catch him in front the television, watching His favorite football game.

(Hab. 3:3) God came from Teman, and the Holy One from Mount Paran. Selah. His glory covered the heavens, and the earth was full of his praise.

Moses taught (in Deuteronomy) that the blessings would come upon you and overtake you if, you would be obedient to God's commands.

(Deut. 28:2) And all these blessings shall come on thee, and overtake thee, if thou shalt hearken unto the voice of the LORD thy God.

Now, if the blessings are overtaking you, the implication is that you are headed in a direction. This speaks of the spiritual direction of your life. There are many verses that speak of drawing near to God, by moving from where you are to where God is. God's throne is in the "sides of the north." To draw near to God, is to draw near to His judgment seat in humility, acknowledging our sin, and throwing yourself on His available mercy. So, if you are drawing near to God in the (spiritual) North, then the blessing coming upon you come from the (figurative) South. The scriptures speak of the South as representing blessing and favor. The lesson is that if you will seek God's throne (figurate north) in your life, the blessings (from the figurative south) will come upon you. SO, if you are in need of blessing or are facing a deficit of God's goodness in your life, then humble yourself and seek His judgment in your situation, and the blessing will be in the forecast for you tomorrow!

Earth, air, fire, and water: Another primary influence on the earth's weather is the sun. The scriptures teach the analogy here, that God is light; He is our sun and shield. The sun is symbolic of God the Father, even as water is a symbol of God the Son, and wind that of God the Holy Spirit. This is also analogous to man because he is made in God's image. The air represents man's spirit, the water speaks of man's soul, and the earth of man's flesh.

(1 John 1:5) This then is the message which we have heard of him, and declare unto you, that God is light, and in him is no darkness at all.

(Psa 84:11) For the LORD God [is] a sun and shield: the LORD will give grace and glory: no good [thing] will he withhold from them that walk uprightly.

It is interesting to note, that the sun gives the sky its blue color. Streams of charged particles (called the solar winds) hurtle toward the earth at a rate of 220 to 500 miles per second, reaching our atmosphere in an astonishing three and a half days. These light waves create the azure hue of the sky and otherwise, shape the earth's climate. Without the warmth of the sun, the earth would be a desolate ball of ice tumbling through space.

God, as light, represents the nurturing aspect of His character. Blue, scripturally, is a type of Christ's incarnation and God's grace. He sends Himself (light) into the earth and the effect is to manifest the color blue in the sky; thus, representing and prefiguring the incarnation and condescension of Christ and His grace. This grace is the effect of Father's affection (His warmth, the sun) upon man's human spirit (the air -- pneuma), causing him to take on the character of that light as it radiates from him. The door of the temple, the ephod, and many of the hangings and fasteners in the tabernacle of Moses were blue. These are all a type of Christ and the character of the Father reflected in man.

The earth's weather processes are reactions to the warmth or, lack of warmth from the sun. Every activity of man's spirit, soul, and body is a direct response to God's nature. God is light, and as He shines upon man, He is reflected in those who receive him. The church is spoken of as "sun clothed woman" reflecting the love of God and the glory of God in the earth. Just as the sun's rays are constant in shining upon the earth, so the Father's love is constant and unchanging.

> *(Rev 12:1) And there appeared a great wonder in heaven; a woman clothed with the sun, and the moon under her feet, and upon her head a crown of twelve stars.*

We must note that, the sun's light does not shine over us all the time. This is because, where there is no shadow of turning in the Father, the earth, representing man is continually turning and rotating away from the sun's warmth. When God seems far away, it is because we have turned from Him, not because He has turned from us. The orbit of our life often finds us straying from the warmth of the Father's affection, and the result is blight, cold, and barrenness.

There are also false lights that display far from the sun, but nonetheless, are visible from earth. Streams of hydrogen ions create a sort of electric current that circles the earth, with electrons moving west to east, and protons moving east to west. Some of the charged particles flowing away from the sun never reach the earth. They move back and forth between the sun and the earth, in what is known as the Van Allen Belts. Sometimes when the sun's energy is weakest on the dark side of the earth, some of these particles escape, and are drawn into the ionosphere, where they collide with earth's ions, generating tremendous amounts of energy. These phenomena generate static filled radio transmissions, or the skylights, known as aurora borealis. This speaks of spiritual influences, that masquerade as coming from God, but only produce "white noise" or spiritual confusion that makes it difficult to have clarity in our understanding of God's will for our lives.

Where the Father is concerned: At a point furthest from His affection, confusing lights or deceiving spirits are in evidence, and the clear voice of the Father is drowned out by the spiritual static of the prince of this world. Jesus said that His sheep knew His voice and would not follow another. Sheep never stray far from the shepherd. As you learn to live out of your sheep nature before God, you need not live in fear of falling into error. The false lights are overcome by the strength and brightness of Christ's influence in your life.

> *(John 10:5) And a stranger will they not follow but will flee from him; for they know not the voice of strangers.*

More on the seasons of your life as a Christian: The earth's orbit around the sun, the moon's orbit around the earth, and the rotation of the earth on its axis all influence the angle at which the sun's light hits the earth's surface. They create the four seasons and our daily weather patterns.

Paul taught men to be "instant in season, and out of season". The preacher declared, that "To everything there is a season."

> *(Eccles. 3:1) To everything [there is] a season, and a time to every purpose under the heaven.*

Again, the primary Christian graces are listed (in Galatians 5:22, 23) as fruits of the Spirit. Why not list them as works? Because if they are produced by works, then it is up to you to make yourself godly. But because they are fruit, you know that these graces are not produced by your willpower since trees don't have a will. They are produced as the tree is placed in an environment conducive to bringing a harvest, and then, only in season. If you don't understand this, then you will fall under needless condemnation, time and again, when these respective fruits fall out of season in your life.

There will be times when the fruit of love will come easily. At other times, you will strive to walk in love and find only barren branches. Perhaps, that is when the fruit of patience is in harvest in your life. Rather than flagellating yourself with some religious condemnation, stop and consider the seasons of your spiritual life, and just why you might be experiencing the difficulty before you.

Whether the season of your life is stormy and bleak or mild and pleasant, understand that season is directly influenced by your posture or position, with regard to the Father. Trees leave off producing fruit, as the earth leans in its axis, away from the sun. There will be times when you are not as close to the Father as you are at other times. Understand this is part of the cyclical nature of the Christian walk, and don't despair or give up. The writer of Hebrews indicated that Moses understood the seasonal nature of spiritual life, choosing persecution rather than the temporary pleasures of sin.

CHAPTER FIVE: BRINGING THE RAINS OF THE SPIRIT

The New Testament word for spirit is "pneuma", which is also the Greek word for wind. The Hebrew word is "Ruach", which is the word used to express what happened when God breathed into man and he became a living soul.

> *(Gen. 2:7) And the LORD God formed man [of] the dust of the ground, and breathed into his nostrils the breath of life, and man became a living soul.*

In the dialog that Jesus conducted with Nicodemus, He insisted that a man must be born again. When Nicodemus questions these, Jesus uses a meteorological reference to describe the character of one who is "born of the Spirit" or "born of the wind".

> *(John 3:8) The wind bloweth where it listeth, and thou hearest the sound thereof, but canst not tell whence it cometh, and whither it goeth: so is every one that is born of the Spirit.*

If you want to understand the life of the Spirit, then it is incumbent upon you to understand the nature of the wind. There are processes at work, on the inside of you, that a study of the wind will give you better understanding. When Jesus speaks of the wind, He is speaking of something of Himself on the inside of you. Where do winds come from? The wind originates from the effect of the sun's heat upon the earth. The warmth of the sun speaks to us of the love of the Father. The Father's love comes upon us and causes our spirits to stir and interact with His kingdom. The sun creates the wind because it warms the planet unevenly. The equatorial regions receive more heat than the poles. As the sun heats the tropics, the warm air from the region rises and moves toward the poles, where it cools and sinks again. Rising and falling masses of warm and cool air create the wind as warm air moves to equalize the cold air. Without the wind, the sun's heat would make the tropics unbearably warm while leaving the poles frigid. Without the wind, the rain would fall constantly over the oceans while the land remained dry. All of these things speak to us, metaphorically, regarding our relationship with God and our relationship with those around us. God's Spirit moves in a current in our lives; in fact, Isa. 11:1-3 reveals there are actually seven currents of God's Spirit at work around us at all times.

> *(Isa. 11:1-3) And there shall come forth a rod out of the stem of Jesse, and a Branch shall grow out of his roots: 2 And the*

spirit of the LORD shall rest upon Him, the spirit of wisdom and understanding, the spirit of counsel and might, the spirit of knowledge and of the fear of the LORD; 3 And shall make Him of quick understanding in the fear of the LORD: and He shall not judge after the sight of His eyes, neither reprove after the hearing of His ears.

Again, these seven spirits are typified by the seven jet streams (or winds) that generate natural weather. They are, in order:

1. The Spirit of the Lord
2. The Spirit of Wisdom
3. The Spirit of Understanding
4. The Spirit of Counsel
5. The Spirit of Might
6. The Spirit of Knowledge
7. The Spirit of the Fear of the Lord

The warmth of the sun draws moisture from the earth's oceans to form clouds and distribute the rain through our eco-system. The oceans represent the realm of darkness and lost humanity.

(Isa. 57:20) But the wicked are like the troubled sea, when it cannot rest, whose waters cast up mire and dirt.

Conversely, it then follows, if the sea represents lost humanity, then the dry land represents the kingdom of God, and more specifically, the community of the redeemed. Remember the verse where Jesus said that demons, when they are expelled, go about in dry places looking for a place of habitation? Demons are always on the hunt to assault and bring down a believer. They seek the dry places because that is where they find their enemy.

> *(Luke 11:24) When the unclean spirit is gone out of a man, he walketh through dry places, seeking rest; and finding none, he saith: "I will return unto my house whence I came out."*

It is important to note, that the winds have an influence on both the land and the sea. God rains on the just and on the unjust. The wind, which is a type of the Holy Spirit, brings the rains of God's blessing on both the dry land and the oceans alike. He rains on the just and the unjust, that His goodness might draw the sinner to repentance.

> *(Rom. 2:4) knowing that the goodness of God leadeth thee to repentance*

> *(Matt. 5:45) That ye may be the children of your Father which is in heaven: for He maketh His sun to rise on the evil and on the good, and sendeth rain on the just and on the unjust.*

As the sun also warms the ocean, the air fills with moisture that rises and creates storm clouds. We will show that clouds represent people. Some clouds speak to us of those with anointing and the rain of God in them. Others are clouds without water (word), that we should avoid. As clouds form, then storms are generated. Just as clouds carry moisture, at times, some people and ministries become carriers of the glory of God. Initially, storms generally move west and generate energy in the atmosphere, pushing up the tropopause, where the warm air is moved (by the winds) toward the poles. In this process, clouds are formed that distribute moisture throughout the earth. The moisture is the rain of God, the Spirit of God being poured out into low-pressure zones. The word for humility means to "go low". The word "Jordan" means "the going low place". These low-pressure zones speak to us of the posture of humility. As you "go low" in the challenges of life, thus adopting humility as your response to pressure, then the seven spirits of God bend low and empty their contents upon your life.

The clouds represent the saints of God, redeemed out of the world. The sun (representing Father's affection) warms the ocean, just as God's love, poured in behalf of lost humanity, draw us to Him. The warmth of the sun draws the moisture out of the ocean, up into the atmosphere (the Pneuma/Spirit of God), where they form into moisture-laden clouds. The sun's warmth (Father's affection) draws water (man's soul) out, purifying it in the process, and forming clouds. The saints are spoken of in scriptures as clouds or water drawn out of the ocean, purified and prepared to pour out of themselves.

> *(Zec. 10:1) Ask ye of the LORD rain in the time of the latter rain; [so] the LORD shall make bright clouds, and give them showers of rain, to every one grass in the field.*

> *(Heb. 12:1) Wherefore seeing we also are compassed about with so great a cloud of witnesses, let us lay aside every weight, and the sin which doth so easily beset [us], and let us run with patience the race that is set before us.*

> *(Matt. 24:30) And then shall appear the sign of the Son of man in heaven, and then shall all the tribes of the earth*

mourn, and they shall see the Son of man coming in the clouds of heaven with power and great glory.

(Mark 13:26) And then shall they see the Son of man coming in the clouds with great power and glory.

What is the glory? Col. 1:26, 27 says that the glory is Christ in us. Where, then, is His appearing? Firstly, His appearing is in us. This is not to reject the physical return of Jesus, but look at the words of Paul that describe Jesus coming IN US before He comes FOR US.

(2 Thess. 1:10) When He shall come to be glorified in his saints, and to be admired in all them that believe (because our testimony among you was believed) in that day.

The atmosphere speaks of the realm of the Spirit: both IN US and AROUND US. Clouds inhabit the atmosphere or the "pneuma". Remember, "The heavens declare the glory of God". The atmosphere is representative of the Spirit of God over all the earth and humanity. By understanding the processes at work in the atmosphere, you can learn spiritual principles at work in you and around you, and thus arrive at a spiritual forecast of your life. In fact, by a posture of humility, you can provoke the spirits of God to pour out in your life.

The earth's atmosphere weighs some five million billion (or 5 quadrillion) tons and exerts pressure on humans at about fifteen pounds per spare inch. It reaches 18,000 miles up but, in comparing earth to an orange, its comparable thickness is that of an orange peel. The air is 78% nitrogen, 21% oxygen, argon, carbon dioxide, neon, helium, methane, krypton, hydrogen, nitrous oxide, and xenon. The outer atmosphere contains less stable gasses, like ozone and radon.

The atmosphere represents the Holy Spirit (the Pneuma). God created the heavens with different levels. Paul spoke of the third heaven, implying a first and a second also. Most weather takes place in the first layer of our atmosphere, known as the tropopause. The word "tropopause" means "to mix". This would be analogous to the first heaven and is the realm of spiritual warfare. This is a place of MIXTURE where human spirits, demon spirits, angels, and God's Spirit all operate according to various factors in our lives. Satan is called the "prince of the power of the air." The Greek word for air describes the lower atmosphere: The Peoples New Testament (PNT) suggests:

> *(Eph 2:2) The prince of the power of the air. Called elsewhere the prince of this world, Satan...*

Why he is called "prince of the power of the air" is not certain, but various explanations are given. It is, probably since Satan's subtle influences and whisperings pervade and come upon us, unconsciously, as the vital air we breathe. The Jews held that the atmosphere was the abode of evil angels. Jacob saw this activity in a vision at Bethel.

> *(Gen. 28:12) And he dreamed, and behold a ladder set up on the earth, and the top of it reached to heaven: and behold the angels of God ascending and descending on it.*

Above this lower turbulent layer of air, is the stratosphere (this means "to smooth out"). It is as far as thirty miles above the surface. The high winds (called jet streams) in this layer blow horizontally, carrying dust, volcanic ash, and acid rain thousands of miles around the globe. The winds here, are dry and clouds are rare. Here, the high concentration of ozone warms the atmosphere, by trapping the reflected heat from the earth. The seven jet streams speak of the "seven spirits of God" that flow in the stratosphere (the second heaven), influencing and shaping the "pneuma" or spiritual interactions in the lower realm (the first heaven or troposphere).

So, you see, in the natural realm, that the air is constantly moving: warm air is rising and cool air is descending. Circulation of air is affected by the land, the oceans, sun, gravity, and the rotation of the earth. The interplay of these forces creates the effects, we know as the weather. Likewise, the interplay of the Spiritual forces, which these natural energies typify, creates the spiritual effects that make up the numinous atmosphere of your life. Comparing the natural atmosphere of the earth with the spiritual atmosphere of your life: It can be observed that you must pierce the first heaven, where the warfare with Satan rages, and go past the MIXTURE with all it turbulence, in order to enter into the rarified atmosphere of the heavenlies.

> *(Act 14:22) confirming the souls of the disciples [and] exhorting them to continue in the faith, and that we must through much tribulation enter into the kingdom of God.*

Acts 14:22 says it is through MUCH TRIBULATION (the spiritual first heaven, analogous to the TROPOSPHERE) to connect with the kingdom of God (the stratosphere, seven spirits of God, the Jet Streams). It is here, in the Stratosphere, that the seven jet streams (corresponding to the Seven Spirits of God) brood over the earth (over the realm of principalities and powers) to bring about God's purpose in your life.

It is interesting to note that the word "stratosphere" is in the same word group as "strategy". God's Spirit rules (strategizes) over all, dictating the TACTICS of spiritual activity and warfare in the lower, first heaven (troposphere). In order to penetrate into the second heaven, we must pierce the mixture of forces in the first heaven (human spirits, demon spirits, angels, etc.). Then, and only then, can we rise above into commiseration with God, in a pure sense, being SEATED with Him in heavenly places, far above the lower ruling powers.

Dealing with the pressures of life: The flowing air pockets of high- and low-pressure in our weather system are called cells. These pressure cells constantly vie with each other to equalize the earth's temperature. High-pressure generally offers clear skies and good weather and the air becomes stable. No one likes pressure, but it is through this pressure in our spiritual lives, and through the warfare, that you enter into the Kingdom of God. Again, Paul exhorted fledgling churches that through "much tribulation", they would enter into the Kingdom of God. The word tribulation indicates great pressure.

This incredulous value placed on the pressures of life is reflected in Jesus' teachings to rejoice in the midst of persecution. It is also in Paul's exhortation, to greatly rejoice in seasons of "manifold temptations." When you are under pressure, you are pressing into the kingdom as the following example illustrates:

High-pressure systems always move towards low-pressure systems. Highs form at the poles because cool air compresses, sinks toward the surface, pushing the wind toward the equator. In the horse latitudes (in the Sargasso Sea), the sun warms the oceans. As the vapor warms, the air rises and is condensed out over the equator. The air becomes dense, falls back to earth as it is warmed by compression, then the amount of humidity in the air drops. Deserts like the Sahara, the Arabian, Kalahari, the Southwestern U.S., and the Great Victoria Desert in Australia; are located in these latitudes. These are areas where there is little or no weather change and, therefore, desolate. Spiritually speaking, this is a reference to repentance. The Psalmist stated, "God shall hear and afflict ... because they have no changes. Therefore, they fear not the Lord." If low-pressure systems speak to us of humility, high-pressure systems represent pride and stubbornness. You must break through the pride of life to find the place of humility where God's jet streams, His seven spirits are attracted.

Highs and lows are sometimes called cyclones. The word cyclone means "to whirl". In the northern hemisphere, high-pressure areas rotate clockwise while lows rotate counterclockwise. When a high- and a low-pressure cell meet, the air is very turbulent as they seek to equalize the pressure. When the spirit of pride and the spirit of humility clash, there is great upheaval until one or the other prevails. Does this explain the spiritual backdrop of turbulence in your life, in times past?

These pockets of air circulate according to a convection process. Convection transfers energy from one place to another. In the case of cells, they warm and rise until they reach the same density of the air to which they have risen. As we ascend in Christ, through the renewing of our mind and maturing in Him, we also take on His character and spiritual composition -- as the low-pressure system equalizes with the high-pressure system.

More detail on Jet Streams: At this point, the cooled air falls back toward earth, around a rising column of warm air.

As this moisture-laden air is cooling it forms the "afternoon thermals" that water the earth in climates, such as the Deep South in the U.S. Then, there is a constant exchange taking place: of warm stale air in the lower atmosphere, with the cool clean air in the upper atmosphere. Some, of the energy of these rising currents, are carried around the world by winds tunnels called, jet streams.

Much of what we know about the weather, was discovered during the world wars with the advent of high altitude flying. During World War Two, the jet stream was a military secret. It was first used by the Japanese to launch bomb-carrying balloons across five thousand miles of ocean to the U.S. Only nine hundred, of the nine thousand balloons, reached the U.S., doing little harm.

These jet streams flow six to thirty miles above the earth where warm and cold air masses meet along the edge of the lower atmosphere. There is a total of seven jet streams that circle the globe. These tunnels of air are massive, measuring several hundred miles wide, and two to three miles deep. At the outer edges, the air travels about fifty mph. At the center of a jet stream, the pace quickens to as much as three hundred mph. Despite their power and speed jet streams travel silently, because, unlike air closer to the surface, they are not obstruct them. The air is also thinner, thus reducing wind resistance and energy. Just because you don't hear anything, doesn't mean that God isn't at work in your life by His Spirit.

> *(Isa. 11:2) And the Spirit of the LORD shall rest upon him, the spirit of wisdom and understanding, the spirit of counsel and might, the spirit of knowledge and of the fear of the LORD.*

Again, it is revealing to note, that there are Seven Spirits of God mentioned in the Scriptures. These correspond to the seven jet streams. Speaking through Isaiah, the Lord revealed these spirits as: the spirit of Lord, the spirit of wisdom, the spirit of understanding, the spirit of counsel, the spirit of might, the spirit of knowledge, and of the fear of the Lord. John, the revelator, gave salutations from these seven spirits, before the throne of God.

Low-pressure areas form, at points under a jet stream's most rapid current. The air is pushed out into the lower atmosphere below, forming a low-pressure area directly under the jet stream. The warm air rises and cools forming rain clouds. Joel prophesied about the Lord pouring out His Spirit on all flesh as the rain upon the earth. Looking into the conditions for natural rain to pour out will give insight into a spiritual rain being powered out in your life.

The prophet Zechariah prophesied that a rain of God's Spirit would come wherein the Lord would form "bright clouds ... giving showers of rain to everyone". As we have already seen, these clouds represent souls drawn out from lost humanity, by the warmth of Father's affection, even as water is drawn from the sea by the warmth of the sun. What do these clouds, these redeemed souls bring upon the earth? They bring the communication of the word of God represented by outpoured rain. You see, revival doesn't just happen. It comes through a process involving various elements, including the human element, the instrumentality of a repentant, humble remnant who are willing servants of the purpose of God.

Just as a weatherman can identify a specific jet stream that has produced a rain bearing weather cell, it is also possible to determine which of the Seven Spirits of God precipitated various outpourings of God through revivals of religion throughout history.

CHAPTER SIX: BRINGING THE RAINS OF GOD INTO YOUR LIFE

God formed and fashioned our outward climate (the weather system of the earth), to reflect the inward climate of our spiritual environment. It is predictable, and unlike the natural weather, it can be influenced and even provoked in foreseeable ways – to our benefit and blessing. We are going to look at the book of Acts and see where the seven Spirits of God began to pour out, and why. We are going to see that the "Jet Streams of God" pour out upon us at times and in particular seasons. We will also see that they do so IN THE ORDER revealed in the scriptures, specifically in Isaiah 11:1-3:

> *(Isa. 11:1-3) And there shall come forth a rod out of the stem of Jesse and a branch shall grow out of his roots: 2And the 1) Spirit of the LORD shall rest upon Him, 2) the spirit of*

wisdom, and 3) understanding, the 4) spirit of counsel, and 5) might, the 6) spirit of knowledge, and of the 7) fear of the LORD; 3 And shall make Him of quick understanding in the fear of the LORD: and He shall not judge after the sight of his eyes, neither reprove after the hearing of His ears.

Now, when you look at this list that God hands down to us through Isaiah, the first we see is the Spirit of the Lord. However, you have to realize that this is a top-down revelation, from God's standpoint. He mentions the Spirit of the Lord because it is the first one that would occur to Him, based on who He is. When we are (metaphorically) looking up to God we don't see the first Spirit listed – the Spirit of the Lord)

Rather we see the last one – the Spirit of the FEAR of the LORD. There are three different mentions of this by way of confirmation in the poetical books:

(Psa 111:10) The fear of the LORD [is] the beginning of wisdom. A good understanding have all they that do [His commandments]; His praise endureth forever.

(Pro 1:7) The fear of the LORD [is] the beginning of knowledge: [but] fools despise wisdom and instruction.

(Pro 9:10) The fear of the LORD [is] the beginning of wisdom: and the knowledge of the holy [is] understanding.

The Spirit of the fear of the Lord: The fear of the Lord is not a beginning for God the Father, but it is a beginning for us. As we encounter the fear of the Lord, it becomes the entry point into experiencing the full bandwidth of who God is, and who He wants to be in our lives. If you can, picture this as a ladder with the Spirit of the Lord at the top and the Spirit of the Fear of the Lord as the bottom rung. The lowest rung constituting the entry point where we begin to learn of God. We come to Him through the Spirit of the fear of the Lord, which acts as the initiator of our relationship with Him. The fear of the Lord is the activator that establishes, in our lives and our hearts, our need of a Savior.

Once the Spirit of the Fear of the Lord is activated in our life what is our greatest need? We need to learn and come to God through teaching of the scripture facilitated by the next Spirit of the Lord (in our list in Isaiah) – the Spirit of KNOWLEDGE.

The Spirit of Knowledge: Fear of any kind is always accompanied by ignorance. We instinctively fear what we do not know. The Hebrew word here, in the passage in Isaiah, is "Daath" and it means to "know by experience…" This is different than the general kind of academic knowledge we think of in our Western Culture. God's autonomic response when He sees that we fear and reverence Him, is to increase our experience of His presence and His person. This word is also the word describing sexual intimacy or knowing a partner in the sexual experience. Therefore, there is a relational component in this word implying intimacy and mutual fellowship.

This kind of knowledge, which flows out of experience and not concept, reveals a common distinction between Western-Culture (that is influenced by Greco-Roman philosophy) and the culture of the ancient world. To a person in ancient times, there was not the sense of KNOWING something – unless it was experienced. Hence the Psalmist says:

(Psa 34:8) O taste and see that the LORD [is] good: blessed, [is] the man [that] trusteth in Him.

To the mind of the ancient, occidental Hebrew (or person of another culture), you do not KNOW God is good until you TASTE, and SEE, and EXPERIENCE that He is good. The apostle Paul instinctively understood this fact of human nature – and geared his entire gospel strategy around it:

(1Co 2:4) And my speech and my preaching [was] not with enticing words of man's wisdom, but in demonstration of the Spirit and of power.

The apostle Paul says, in another place, that he speaks wisdom to those who are wise; with everyone else, he only preaches the demonstration of the cross. In our modern-day religious culture, we tend to focus on talking about God, as contrasted by demonstrating the power of God, the wisdom of God and the knowledge of God. God has called us to be demonstrators, not religious academics. Therefore, the knowledge of God (brought by the spirit of the knowledge of God) is something much more visceral and impactful than we can ever know from a simple, dry, religious standpoint.

The Spirit of Might: What does the Spirit of the knowledge of God precede? The fear of the Lord brings us to seek out the knowledge of God, and we experience Him and know that He is good. With the knowledge of God, we begin to be opened to those opportunities, to see the might and power of God producing in our lives that which is promised.

Therefore, after the Spirit of the knowledge of God, we are ushered or we ascend into the Spirit of might. The word of "might" here, contains a meaning in the original Hebrew that is easily overlooked, by those of us with analytical minds. The word "might" indeed, does mean mighty and powerful, but it includes a descriptive characteristic of being mighty and powerful in an impetuous way.

Being impetuous implies acting, without hesitation. If you are going to act without hesitation, you won't have time to assess – in your mind, your logic, or your intellect – the practicality of what you are about to do. Men and women of great boldness in healing and miracle ministry, often act without thinking – even ignoring potential consequences. They often see powerful, over the top miracles produced, as a result. If you want to see the light of God demonstrated in your life, you're not going to be able to live a life of hesitation, analysis, or refusal to take risks. The fear of the Lord will disincentivize you, regarding other considerations like disobeying God. Then, the knowledge of the Lord will inform you concerning the basis of God's promises. The Spirit of the might of God will provoke you to act on what you know, in honor of God, to see miracles come to pass.

The Spirit of Counsel: After the Spirit of might, we find the Spirit of counsel listed. In fact, the Spirit of counsel is mentioned, along with (in the same sentence and phrase as) the spirit of might. Why must we have the Spirit of counsel in tandem, or in connection with, the Spirit of might? Consider the following:

> *(Matt. 22:15) Then went the Pharisees and took counsel how they might entangle Him in [His] talk.*

> *(Matt. 27:1, 7) 1 When the morning was come, all the chief priests and elders of the people took counsel against Jesus to*

put him to death: ... 7 and they took counsel and bought with them the potter's field, to bury strangers in.

(Mark 3:6) And the Pharisees went forth, and straightway took counsel with the Herodians against Him, how they might destroy Him.

(John 11:53) Then, from that day forth, they took counsel together for to put Him to death.

(Act 5:33) When they heard [that], they were cut [to the heart] and took counsel to slay them.

(Act 9:23) And after that, many days were fulfilled, the Jews took counsel to kill Him.

Every time Jesus, one of the disciples, or one of the apostles moved in power or produced miracles when the Spirit of might was made manifest; the enemies of the cross and enemies of the gospel would come together in wicked counsel against the purposes of God. When the enemy is taking counsel against you, God releases the spirit of counsel to counteract, confound, and confuse the counsels of the enemy.

The Spirit of Understanding: When the fear of the Lord comes and the Spirit of the fear of the Lord, the knowledge of God is poured out, bringing the testimony of His might. When the might of God is manifested, your enemies will take counsel to damage you – in response to which, God will pour out the Spirit of His counsel, to confound all their plans. What Spirit of the Lord comes next? The Spirit of understanding. When you begin to realize that you and God are a majority – in spite of the all-out efforts of the enemy, to impede and destroy the works of your hands – THEN UNDERSTANDING begins to dawn on just who you are in Christ, and who He is in you, on the earth. Remember now, that the Seven Spirits of God and like a ladder. You are ascending into a deeper, and more profound revelation of who He is in your life, and what it means to belong to Him and walk into the kingdom. When you experience the fear of the Lord, gain the knowledge of God, see the might of God manifested, and the counsel of God defeating your enemies; then comes an ASCENSION MOMENT: an epiphany, which you understand, that God is with you and DEFEAT IS NOT AN OPTION.

The Spirit of Wisdom: When you come to this place and begin to experience the overwhelming favor of God in your life, many people shipwreck right here. They are so scarred by years of failure and frustration that, when they hit their stride in the kingdom, and everything they do is as effective as if God said it or did it, they begin to make unwise and harmful decisions. Those choices dismantle their standing in God and His favor. To combat this, the WISDOM OF GOD is immediately available; prompting you not to stop where you are, but go on to a deeper realization of God's purposes in your life. This is a point that Hosea spoke of, regarding the need to MAKE A CHOICE, to FOLLOW ON, to know the Lord – even after His power is manifest as an on-tap resource in your life.

(Hos. 6:3) Then, shall we know, [if] we follow on to know the LORD: His going forth is prepared as the morning, and He shall come unto us as the rain, as the latter [and] former rain unto the earth.

There will come a point in your life, if you stay sensitive to the Holy Spirit, that everything you say and do will become as effective as if God said it or did it. Your prayers will be answered. Your body will be healed. Your finances will be provided. You will see great blessing upon your own life. You will be a conduit of blessing, power, and the favor of God poured out to others. Do not allow this to become a stopping place. Many people are only incentivized by the sense of their need, and wanting to get prayers answered. These shallow believers come to a place of seeing answers and simply stop growing.

Just because you can pray a prayer and get an answer, doesn't mean you have arrived. You must press into the wisdom of God, not just seeing God's acts, but learning His ways. Moses understood this:

> *(Psa 103:7) He [God] made known his ways unto Moses, His acts unto the children of Israel.*

The wisdom of God turns all your question marks into exclamation points if you have the boldness to hear, and a teachable heart. It is amazing that many people who walk in miracles, are some of the least teachable and least revelation-filled believers that you will ever meet. They experienced entitlement in God and lost their spiritual appetite. Do not allow this to happen to you, but keep pressing into His wisdom, and the Spirit of wisdom, that is available to pour out in your life.

The Spirit of the Lord: Finally we come to the "Spirit of the Lord". This is God's primary, raw and native affectation by which He reveals Himself to us. Many times we don't see God's Lordship, but it is always around us, in every circumstance and transaction of life. Just because a situation in your life may not look like God is in control, doesn't mean that He isn't. God works on a timetable different from you. God does not have any impatience, unbelief, or confusion. He has a "Ways and Means Committee" to bring breakthrough in your life. If you will be patient and allow Him to BRING YOU THROUGH the PROCESS (of REVEALING the FULL BANDWIDTH of His character seen in the Seven Spirits of God), then you will ascend into a place where you will rule in life NOW. The writer of the book of Revelation says that you will rule with a rod of unbending spiritual authority. It is available and experiential – if you will submit to the process.

> *(Rev. 2:26-27) And he that overcometh, and keepeth my works unto the end, to him will I give power over the nations. 27and he shall rule them with a rod of iron; as the vessels of a potter shall they be broken to shivers: even as I received of My Father.*

The Pattern in the Book of Acts: How do we cooperate with God in this process? How do we invoke the Spirit of the fear of the Lord and the respective WINDS of God that expose us to His greatness in our lives? First of all, remember that this is something on the inside of you. This is not an external process. Whatever the kingdom is, it is on the INSIDE OF YOU (Luke 17: 20, 21). The Spirit of God can be invoked and activated by presenting Him with the "low place" of humility, as your baseline spiritual environment and response to His presence. It is also important to know, that these Seven Spirits or winds of God operate in an identifiable order, as revealed in Isa. 11:1-3. By the way of example, compare the order of the Spirits of God as mentioned in Isaiah with how these same

Spirits of God were poured out in the book of Acts, beginning with Ananias and Sapphira.

Ananias and his wife die for lying to the Holy Spirit and… great fear came upon all the church. This is the outpouring of the Spirit of the Fear of the Lord. What is next? The Spirit of Knowledge and then the Spirit of Might.

> *(Acts 5:11) great fear came upon all the church, and upon as many as heard these things, multitudes were added to the Lord (through Preaching – the Spirit of the Knowledge of the Lord:*

> *(Acts 5:14) and believers were the more added to the Lord, multitudes both of men and women.*

Multitudes were healed; Peter's shadow even produces miracles (Spirit of Might).

> *(Acts 5:15) Insomuch that they brought forth the sick into the streets, and laid them on beds and couches, that at the least the shadow of Peter passing by might overshadow some of them.*

The high priest and the leaders conspire (take counsel) and imprison Peter and others.

> *(Acts 5:17-18) Then the high priest rose up, and all they that were with him, (which is the sect of the Sadducees,) and were filled with indignation, 18and laid their hands on the apostles, and put them in the common prison.*

The Spirit of Counsel comes (as we see in Acts 5:29-33) and Peter replies to their evil counsel completely shutting their mouths and cutting them to the heart.

(Acts 5:29-32) Then Peter and the other apostles answered and said: "we ought to obey God rather than men. 30The God of our fathers raised up Jesus, whom ye slew and hanged on a tree. 31Him hath God exalted with his right hand to be a Prince and a Saviour, for to give repentance to Israel and forgiveness of sins. 32And we are his witnesses of these things; and so is also the Holy Ghost, whom God hath given to them that obey him". 33When they heard that, they were cut to the heart...

The disciples are beaten, but they leave rejoicing because they know, and come to UNDERSTAND, that God rules over all; with Him by their side, they are a majority (Spirit of Understanding.) Acts 5:41 and they departed from the presence of the council, rejoicing that they were counted worthy to suffer shame for His name.

In the aftermath of this great victory, a great controversy arises which could have destroyed the church with strife from within. God brings the outpouring of the Spirit of Wisdom, and the problem is solved with the appointment of the seven deacons to direct the resources of the foundling early church.

(Acts 6:1-5) And in those days, when the number of the disciples was multiplied, there arose a murmuring of the Grecians against the Hebrews, because their widows were neglected in the daily ministration. 2Then the twelve called the multitude of the disciples unto them, and said: "It is not reason that we should leave the word of God, and serve tables. 3Wherefore, brethren, look ye out among you seven men of honest report, full of the Holy Ghost and wisdom, whom we

may appoint over this business. 4But we will give ourselves continually to prayer, and to the ministry of the word." 5And the saying pleased the whole multitude: and they chose Stephen, a man full of faith and of the Holy Ghost, and Philip, and Prochorus, and Nicanor, and Timon, and Parmenas, and Nicolas a proselyte of Antioch.

Then, the word of God increased. How can the word of God increase? What else could possibly go right? The leaders of the early church, have now, fully ascended and experienced the full outpouring of the seven winds of God in their midst.

(Acts 6:7) And the word of God increased, and the number of the disciples multiplied in Jerusalem greatly, and a great company of the priests were obedient to the faith.

The resulting effect was to unleash a sovereign move of the Spirit, which riveted all of human history to the realities of the Cross and the resurrection of Jesus. The Spirit of the Lord was poured out and, even to this day, we are experiencing the benefits.

(Acts 6:7) And the word of God increased, and the number of the disciples multiplied in Jerusalem greatly, and a great company of the priests were obedient to the faith.

We can easily see this pattern in the ancient church. But, you can experience this same outpouring, this spiritual climate shift, in your own life. You can come out of spiritual famine and drought, beginning with the posture of humility that causes the Spirit of the Fear of the Lord as one of God's jet streams to bend low into your life and pour itself out in your behalf. This initiates the process, which with your cooperation, leads the THRONE LIFE of the Spirit of the Lord, that is, the preeminent and primary manifestation of who God is, and who He wants to be in our lives.

CHAPTER SEVEN – IT'S GOING TO RAIN!

In Genesis, we read that after the great flood, God made a promise to Noah never to destroy the earth by water again.

> *(Genesis 9:12-16) And God said, This is the token of the covenant which I make … 13I do set my bow in the cloud, … 14And it shall come to pass, when I bring a cloud over the earth, that the bow shall be seen in the cloud: 15And I will remember my covenant… 16And the bow shall be in the cloud, and I will look upon it, that I may remember the everlasting covenant...*

The bow God speaks of is the rainbow set in the cloud. This is one of the most beautiful phenomena that occurs in our weather system. It speaks almost universally of promise and favor – yet so much more. This "bow" that this verse refers to is exactly the same rainbow you and I commonly see before or after a rain event. Remember that rain is a commonly used metaphor in scripture for the outpouring of God's Spirit and God's blessing. What application then can we make for ourselves in this verse?

Does the Rainbow Have any Meaning For Us? First of all, Jesus said that the dealings of God in Noah's day would foreshadow and parallel the dealings of God in our day. We can study the Noah narrative and extract information about what we, ourselves, can expect in terms of God's dealings in our lives, even on a personal level:

> *(Matthew 24:37) But as the days of Noe were, so shall also the coming of the Son of man be.*

If we accept Jesus' statement in the preceding verse, it is not doing violence to the meaning if we conclude that: just as the Father put a "bow in a cloud" in Noah's day, EVEN SO, He is putting a prophetic "bow in a cloud in our day". There is no indication in the narrative, or subsequent scriptures, that this is exclusive to Noah and not applicable to you and me today, even on a personal level. Paul taught that the people and events recorded in the Old Testament actually foreshadowed things that God is saying to you and me today:

(1 Cor. 10:11) Now all these things happened unto them for ensamples: and they are written for our admonition, upon whom the ends of the world are come (See Rom. 15:4; Col. 2:17; Heb. 8:5; Heb. 10:1).

In other words, Paul claims (in the preceding verses) that the Old Testament record handed down to us, merely foreshadows matters of greater import and substance that

APPLY TO US TODAY. In the cloud then, and in the bow, God is speaking of Himself to us and in us. So what does the BOW (or Rainbow) and the Cloud in Genesis 9 speak to us?

Jude 1:12 tells us that clouds actually speak of people. Even when Jesus speaks of coming in the clouds, we understand He is speaking not merely of natural clouds, but clouds of people (See Mark 14:62; 1 Th. 4:17; Rev. 1:7). See Also Hebrews 12:1 and Jude 1:14 the principle is: FIRST THE NATURAL, then the SPIRITUAL. Therefore, the Father is saying that as He did with Noah in the natural (putting a bow in the cloud), so in our day He is putting a spiritual bow into a spiritual cloud (His people). What does this mean? It is, in fact, a veiled reference to God living inside of us by the Holy Spirit.

A rainbow is made up of light reflected in a prismatic effect through water vapor. Doesn't the scripture tell us that God is light? (See 1 John 1:5). So, God is in us and He is light. What happens to us, as a result? We become what He is; we become "light in the Lord" (See Eph. 5:8; Matt. 5:14; John 8:12). God created natural light to have properties that speak of Himself and of Himself IN US. What are some of the basic properties of light? For the purpose of our teaching, we point out that light, when cast through a prism or in a rainbow, reveals seven colors.

Seven Visible Colors – Seven Spirits of God: If God is light and light refracts seven colors in the visible spectrum we can see with the naked eye, what does that speak to us? Remember in Isa. 11:1-4 the scriptures tell us that there are SEVEN SPIRITS OF GOD. These seven spirits of God, in the order given in the preceding verse, correspond to the seven colors of the rainbow:

Red   —   Spirit of the Lord
Orange   —   Spirit of Wisdom
Yellow —   Spirit of Understanding
Green —   Spirit of Counsel
Blue   —   Spirit of Might
Indigo —   Spirit of Knowledge
Violet —   Spirit of the Fear of the Lord

In short, God is making the point that because He indwells each of us, we (therefore) have the fullness of His character and attributes living in and activated in us, as God goes about the business of BEING GOD IN US! God is light and He is all these things or attributes in us. However, looking deeper, we know that Jesus taught just as God is light, so WE ARE LIGHT (Matt. 5:14). Consequently, the characteristic of light euphemistically portraying God's character and fullness, may also be refracted in our character – as we see Him and become like Him.

What is true in Christ, is true in us: Col. 2:8-9 says that in Christ dwells the fullness of the God-head bodily. Someone might say, "Well, that was Jesus". That isn't what it says; the verse doesn't make that distinction. It is speaking of Jesus of course, but emphasis is on who He is – AS CHRIST– because the Father wants us to know that "CHRIST IN US" (Col. 1:26-29) will manifest in our heart. This, not just as a token presence, but the very fullness of all that He is and all that He is doing, being transacted in us and through us, right now. Therefore, the seven spirits of God are not merely an expression of the ineffable or unknowable things of God; but they rather reveal who He is in us (in our own daily experience) if we will open ourselves and align ourselves with the experience.

The visible spectrum of God's glory: There is coming a shift, that the rainbow in the Noah narrative is indicative and descriptive of, in the last days. God made a promise to Noah (see Gen. 9:12-16), never to destroy the earth by water again. As a confirmation of that promise, He placed a rainbow in a cloud.

Now Jesus said that the last days would be "as the days of Noah" (See Matt. 24:37). When did the last days begin? The last days began with the inauguration of Jesus' ministry (when He was baptized by John in the Jordan).

> *(Matt. 11:12-15) and from the days of John the Baptist until now the kingdom of heaven suffereth violence and the violent take it by force. 13For all the prophets and the law prophesied until John. 14And if ye will receive [it], this is Elias, which was for to come. 15He that hath ears to hear, let him hear (See also Matt. 3:2; Matt. 4:17; Matt. 10:7; Mark 1:15; Luke 21:31).*

God uses the prophetic ministry (such as John the Baptist) to initiate change in the earth. The Angel of Change comes to initiate the change and the prophetic ministry is always the harbinger of these seasons' transition. So, if you believe the scriptures that say the days of the coming of the Son of Man (commencing with the birth of Christ) would be as the days of Noah, then among other things, we can make the following supposition:

> *(1 Cor. 15:46) Howbeit that [was] not first which is spiritual, but that which is natural, and afterward that which is spiritual.*

Noah had a natural rainbow in a natural cloud, as a manifestation of God while, we have a spiritual rainbow in a spiritual cloud. We have shown that clouds are spoken of, in scripture, as a type of PEOPLE (See Mark 14:62; 1 Th. 4:17; Rev. 1:7. Also Heb. 12:1 and Jude 1:14). God is putting something of Himself in us, which is explained and understood, by studying the properties of a rainbow.

Further Understanding of the Rainbow: Again what is a rainbow? The Science Dictionary defines a rainbow as:

> *"An arc-shaped spectrum of light (God is light- 1 John 1:5) seen in the sky opposite the Sun, especially after rain (God's Spirit- Hos. 6:3), caused by the refraction and reflection of sunlight, by droplets of water (Water represents the Word of God see Eph. 5:26) suspended in the air."*

Again, simply put, that a rainbow is a refraction of light. John the Beloved tells us that "God is Light". The rainbow represents a reflection of God Himself in the earth, in us specifically.

> *(1 John 1:5) This then is the message which we have heard of Him and declare unto you, that God is light, and in Him is no darkness at all.*

We've already established that we are the clouds. So a rainbow represents that nature of God, refracting in our lives, as God shines His light into our hearts (See 2 Cor. 4:6). We are light in the Lord and it is intended that we refract or reflect His glory as His clouds. What are clouds? They are made up of water vapor. We have previously shown, that in the scripture, water is a metaphor for the word. Actually, in the scripture, there are clouds (men) with water and clouds without water. A cloud without water cannot create a rainbow – it cannot refract the glory of God.

Clouds without water are unable to refract God's glory: One of the greatest evils the scriptures tell us about, are men and women who are "clouds without water" (See Jude 1:12). What does that mean? A cloud without water is a cloud that cannot refract a rainbow. Spiritually speaking, a cloud without water is a man or woman who does not refract God's nature in the earth. We are in the image of God but aren't reflecting His image. This is false advertising and is a fraud on a cosmic scale.

So, we now understand why God sent a rainbow as a sign of His promise, not to destroy the earth again by flood. He destroyed it in the first place, because of the entrenched evil in men's hearts (See Gen. 6:5). By implication: If God destroyed the earth because of evil in men's hearts, in order to promise NOT to do this again, He must take responsibility to make it possible (through Christ, IN US) so that we can do the OPPOSITE of reflecting evil. He did this by sending Jesus into our hearts to REFRACT THE GLORY OF GOD in our lives, even on a daily basis. We accomplish this refraction by 1) doing what we see the Father do [John 5:19], 2) having no opinion about the consequences of doing #1 [Matt. 7:1], and 3) then, relinquishing the outcome [John 12:24]. This was how Jesus glorified the Father, and it is how you and I reflect the glory of God the Father, to a lost and dying world.

Seven revealed attributes of God in us: The whole point of the rainbow is God committing Himself to remediate the evil in man (by the Cross) and being willing to do whatever was necessary to see Himself reflected IN US – through the indwelling Christ! This is the mandate of the cross of Christ! We saw that the rainbow has seven colors which are, in fact, the visible spectrum of light (God is light). Again, we refer to Isaiah 11:1-4, which tells us there are seven spirits of God that are, in fact, the seven-fold manifestation of God's glory (or visibility in the earth).

Red	–	Spirit of the Lord
Orange	–	Spirit of Wisdom
Yellow	–	Spirit of Understanding
Green	–	Spirit of Counsel
Blue	–	Spirit of Might
Indigo	–	Spirit of Knowledge
Violet	–	Spirit of the Fear of the Lord

We will take each of these aspects of God's nature and explore what they are and how God causes them to be reflected in our life.

Refracting the glory: Let's briefly review what we have emphasized in this chapter:

Jesus taught that the character of the last days would be reflected in the days that Noah lived:

> *(Matthew 24:37) But as the days of Noe were, so shall also the coming of the Son of man be.*

According to the teachings of Jesus, the "last days" began with His own baptism of John in the Jordan.

> *(Matt. 11:12-15) and from the days of John the Baptist until now the kingdom of heaven suffereth violence and the violent take it by force. 13For all the prophets and the law prophesied until John. 14And if ye will receive [it], this is Elias, which was for to come. 15He that hath ears to hear, let him hear.*

We can begin to understand what Noah's day means to us today by comprehending the teaching of Paul, that the natural occurrences in the Old Testament times foreshadow spiritual experiences for those of us in the New Testament time frame.

(1 Cor. 15:46) Howbeit that [was] not first which is spiritual, but that which is natural, and afterward that which is spiritual.

Therefore, looking at Gen. 9 through the lens of 1 Cor. 15:46, we conclude: If Noah had the natural occurrence of a rainbow in a cloud, then the cloud and rainbow must then point to and foreshadow, a spiritual experience available to you and I.

We are God's clouds. The scriptures are replete with typology speaking of men and women as "clouds". (See Mark 14:62; 1 Th. 4:17; Rev. 1:7. Also Hebrews 12:1 and Jude 1:14)

The Rainbow, according to the Scientific Dictionary, is a refraction of light. 1 John 1:5 tells us that GOD IS LIGHT. The rainbow, as a natural phenomenon, expresses to us something about God's nature (Ro. 1:20).

Therefore, the rainbow in the cloud speaks of GOD, IN US. God is purposing to REFRACT something of Himself in us.

The cloud and the rainbow, in the context of Isa. 11:1-4, tell us something of what God wants to establish in us and what He desires that others will see working in, and through us. He is coming in the clouds and He is coming IN US (at all times and in all places) if we will understand and cooperate with Him, at a higher level than we have in times past. Let's look a little deeper at this thought and see if it is scriptural:

1 Thess. 4:16 speaks of the apocalyptic coming of the Lord. This is commonly believed to be the event, by which, God

removes the righteous from the earth and commences the final judgment, leading up to the end of time.

> *(1 Thess. 4:16) For the Lord, Himself, shall descend from heaven with a shout, with the voice of the archangel, and with the trump of God: and the dead in Christ shall rise first.*

Yet, Paul makes another statement about something that will happen, BEFORE those things described in the preceding verse

> *(2 Thess. 1:10) When He shall come to be glorified in his saints, and to be admired in all them that believe (because our testimony among you was believed) in that day.*

How are we to understand these verses, in comparison one to another? One teacher puts it this way: Christ is coming IN US before He comes FOR US! In 2 Thess. 1:10 the word "glorified" is defined as "to be adorned with glory, light, effulgence (light) to be adorned with the out-raying of the Divine." Isn't this a description of what a rainbow does to a cloud? A rainbow ADORNS a cloud. And the Father is purposing to ADORN US....

God's adornment in us: The Rainbow has seven colors. It adorns the cloud with seven colors. There are seven spirits of God that the Father wants to adorn Himself within us.

> *(Isa. 11:1-3) And there shall come forth a rod out of the stem of Jesse, and a Branch shall grow out of his roots: 2And the spirit of the LORD shall rest upon Him, the spirit of wisdom and understanding, the spirit of counsel and might, the spirit of knowledge and of the fear of the LORD; 3And shall make Him of quick understanding in the fear of the LORD: and*

He shall not judge after the sight of His eyes, neither reprove after the hearing of His ears.

Again, the Seven Spirits of God, which also correspond to the seven Jet Streams, we have spoken of throughout this writing, listed in order with the colors of the Rainbow are:

Red   –   Spirit of the Lord
Orange   –   Spirit of Wisdom
Yellow –   Spirit of Understanding
Green   –   Spirit of Counsel
Blue   –   Spirit of Might
Indigo –   Spirit of Knowledge
Violet –   Spirit of the Fear of the Lord

God is reminding HIMSELF not us: Now remember that God didn't put the rainbow in the cloud in Noah's day to remind us of His promise not to destroy the earth. He put the rainbow in the cloud to REMIND HIMSELF (Gen. 9:15).

In other words instead of looking upon the wickedness of man He put a refraction of Himself in man so that He would see HIMSELF in humanity instead of seeing our sinful condition. And based on what He sees, He forebears judgment.

(Gen. 9:15) And I will remember my covenant, which [is] between me and you and every living creature of all flesh, and the waters shall no more become a flood to destroy all flesh.

When you need an answered prayer, a hand of deliverance from God, He doesn't go through your life with a fine scrutiny to see if you are worthy. He simply looks for the refraction of Himself, in you by His Spirit, and then acts on your behalf. Let us then, open our lives to explore and optimize the fullness of God's Spirit, finding it is reflecting in our very person, at a most rudimentary level.

Ascending Jacob's ladder, riding the prevailing winds of God's Spirit:

In Gen. 9:12-15, God revealed the nature of His spirit through the seven hues seen in the prism of a rainbow. Isaiah 11:1-3 further illuminates the special meaning of the rainbow by enumerating for us the Seven Spirits of God. The order in which the color of the rainbow appear is determined by nature. This order corresponds the each color with a specific attribute of God's Spirit as listed in order in the inspired word of God.

The Seven Spirits of God listed in order with the colors of the Rainbow are:

Red — Spirit of the Lord
Orange — Spirit of Wisdom
Yellow — Spirit of Understanding
Green — Spirit of Counsel
Blue — Spirit of Might
Indigo — Spirit of Knowledge
Violet — Spirit of the Fear of the Lord

This is, if you will, a "top-down" revelation of God. Red is the highest color in the arc and violet is the lowest color. We come to know God, first by coming to the "Spirit of the Fear of the Lord". This is the "bottom-up" approach we make to God, which is the reverse of how He reveals Himself in the rainbow.

THE FEAR OF THE LORD:

The Fear of the Lord is the entry point in every person's relationship with God:

(Ps. 19:9) The fear of the LORD [is] clean, enduring forever.

It is in the fear of the Lord we come and receive cleansing. That is our first, felt need when we begin to ascend the seven spirits of God, or Jacob's ladder into an intimate relationship with the Father. THE SPIRIT OF KNOWLEDGE

(Prov. 1:7) The fear of the LORD [is] the beginning of knowledge. (Also Prov. 1:29)

When we embrace the FEAR of the LORD, it deposits us on the cusp of the KNOWLEDGE of the LORD and we begin our ascent into God. We don't leave the Fear of the Lord; actually, it remains the ongoing and upward context for ascending into deeper intimacy with GOD.

THE SPIRIT OF MIGHT

The knowledge of God causes us to ascend into the MIGHT OF GOD. The word might here is "valor, strength, exploits, mighty deeds". Now what does the knowledge of God have to do with "mighty deeds and exploits"? What is the correlation of the Spirit of the Knowledge of God to the Spirit of Might?

(Dan. 11:32) The people that do know their God shall be strong, and do [exploits].

In the original language, this word "know" is often used as a euphemism for "sexual intercourse". So the knowledge here, invokes a picture of intimate discourse with God, as opposed to mere intellectual perception.

THE SPIRIT OF COUNSEL

The Spirit of Counsel and the Spirit of Might are actually

paired together in Isaiah 11:2. It speaks of the "predictions, plans and purposes" of God. These "predictions, plans, and purposes" are what ARISES from the intimacy we come to, as we have ascended in THE SPIRIT OF THE KNOWLEDGE OF GOD, having ACTIVATED THAT KNOWLEDGE, in exploits of faith by THE SPIRIT OF MIGHT.

THE SPIRIT OF UNDERSTANDING

The word "understanding", here, speaks of discernment. It is the ability to grasp and comprehend. It is the natural outflow from the previous four apprehensions of your heart of the Spirit of God. We approach the Father in Godly fear. We become intimately related to Him and come to know Him. Because of that knowledge we act in boldness of faith, demonstrating His might in the earth. Having experienced the power of God and His limitlessness, we then gain comprehension of His counsels, and what His "predictions, plans, and purposes" are. Through His fear, His knowledge, and His might, we then ascend into a grasp of His mind (intellect) and begin to comprehend and have understanding of the scope of who He is in our midst.

THE SPIRIT OF WISDOM

There is a distinction between WISDOM, KNOWLEDGE, and UNDERSTANDING. Knowledge gives us INFORMATION; Understanding gives us COMPREHENSION; Wisdom gives us APPLICATION of what we understand and comprehend. Wisdom tells us WHAT TO DO with WHAT WE KNOW. Wisdom is the apex of the previous five attributes of God's Spirit. He gives us those five (the number of grace) that we might attain to the sixth (His Wisdom). Six is the number of Man.

The first five represent the attributes He gives us in His grace (5) in order that we might attain to the apex or height of human experience (6 – the number of man) possible in God: to walk in His wisdom. And His wisdom is not some neutral principle. 1 Cor. 1:30, 31 tells us that WISDOM IS A PERSON – the MAN / GOD Christ Jesus!

> *(1 Cor. 1:30-31)   30 But of Him are ye in Christ Jesus, who of God is made unto us wisdom, and righteousness, and sanctification, and redemption, 31 that, according as it is written, He that glorieth, let him glory in the Lord.*

THE SPIRIT OF THE LORD

Having ascended from the Fear of the Lord to the Wisdom of God, we then are uniquely enabled to acknowledge HIS LORDSHIP IN OUR LIVES and to ACTIVATE HIS ASCENDENCY, in everything that concerns us. You will never know the FULLNESS of the LORDSHIP OF JESUS CHRIST without ascending, as Jacob did of old in his lifetime, and being changed in nature from a JACOB (SUPPLANTER) TO AN ISRAEL (PRINCE, PRINCIPALITY among NATIONS)

In Conclusion: If you can understand anything about the weather, you can understand MUCH about the dealing of God and the ecosystem of God's Spirit operating in your life. You can predict, anticipate, (and in fact) participate, and provoke the winds of God to produce in your behalf by; your humility, your faith, and your understanding – not just of God's acts, but His ways. You can posture yourself on the blessing side of what you will see God is doing in the earth, and reap the benefits. You have within you, a HOLY GHOST LIGHTNING ROD, which will bring the discharge of God's purposes and promises in your life.

Speaking of lightning, did you know that lightning not only strikes downward but also 5% of the time, it strikes UPWARD. Lightning that strikes upward (upward lightning), is more positively than negatively charged; whereas downward lightning is primarily negatively charged. Positively charged lightning is so rare, it is called "a bolt from the blue..." This is a common metaphor we use for some random occurrence, which we presume, has no predicating condition that we can provoke. Nothing can be further from the truth. Remember when Jesus sent out the disciples and they came back rejoicing because of the miracles and the authority they experienced? Jesus rejoiced with them and explained what they experienced, in the metaphor of a meteorological event.

(Luke 10:18) and He said unto them: "I beheld Satan as lightning fall from heaven".

What the apostles did on the earth, caused Satan to fall from heaven. The power of God, in the apostles, (as they went out obeying God, humbling themselves, thus provoking the autonomic response of God, drawing near on their behalf) caused the powers of the enemy in the heavens, to be discharged by the power of God operating, through the humility of the disciples on the earth. In another place, Jesus describes these very same phenomena, as what we today call "a bolt from the blue":

(Luke 17:24) For as the lightning, that lighteneth out of the one [part] under heaven, shineth unto the other [part] under heaven, so shall also the Son of man be in his day.

A bolt from the blue is a lightning strike that, seemingly, comes out of nowhere. This type of lightning only occurs 5% of the time. The polarity of a bolt from the blue is primarily POSITIVE. Whereas, downward strike lightning is, primarily NEGATIVE in polarity. Here is how scientists describe it:

> *"Unlike the far more common negative lightning, positive lightning originates from the positively charged top of the clouds (generally anvil clouds), rather than the lower portion of the storm. Leaders form in the anvil of the cumulonimbus and may travel horizontally for several miles, before veering towards the ground. A positive lightning bolt can strike anywhere within several miles of the anvil of the thunderstorm, often in areas experiencing clear or only slightly cloudy skies; They are also known as 'bolts from the blue' for this reason. Positive lightning typically makes up less than 5% of all lightning strikes. "*

The difference between "normal" lightning and a "bolt from the blue" is that it is POSITIVE lightning. The positive electronic particles make a circuit with the negative lightning (principality) overhead, and discharges its power, thus creating an open heaven. Have you even noticed how clean the air smells after a lightning storm? The open heaven is not a religious euphemism; it is a reality that can be precipitated by the occasion of your faith, as Jesus said.

> *(Luke 18:8) I tell you that He will avenge them speedily. Nevertheless, when the Son of man cometh, shall He find faith on the earth?*

What is your takeaway from all of this? 1) You can predict the spiritual climate of your life. 2) By your humility, you can provoke the spiritual climate of your life: causing the Seven Spirits of God to bend low into your life, pouring out the beneficial rains of the Spirit upon you. 3) You can ascend into the heavens and become a word laden cloud of God. When this happens, God sees His "bow" refracted in you and remembers His promise to bless YOU. 4) You can discharge the powers and principalities of darkness by the positivity of your obedience, seeing in your life "Satan, as lightning, fall from heaven". The enemy wants us to feel helpless in our situation, as though there is no connection or means to provoke heaven's resources to manifest in our lives. Nothing could be further from the truth. This is what Jesus went to great lengths (in Matt. 16:3) to stress to the Pharisees. The principles and realities of God's power are knowable, and they are responsive to conditions that you and I can set (by our faith), that will produce a predictable outcome of blessing. You are God's bolt from the blue, His cloud filled with promise, His weatherman who will always know what is on the morrow: As you discern – as you CHOOSE TO DISCERN – the face of your "spiritual sky", the immediate spiritual environment, and align with His heart, at that moment, to thenceforth live under an open heaven.

ABOUT THE AUTHOR

Russell Walden is a writer, teacher, and marketplace apostle. Prophet Russ brings a new dimension of personal empowerment to the prophetic through his dynamic and positive anointing. He served for two decades as a full time pastor in the Deep South and as a successful businessman in the mid-west for 15 years. He worked as a denominational leader in Southern Missouri, involved in the supervision of hundreds of churches and ministries. He has flowed in prophetic wisdom and insight for over thirty years. Russ and his wife, Kitty travel throughout the U.S. and around the world preaching, teaching and prophesying as is their mandate. Russ and Kitty's prophetic emphasis is that 'Love Never Fails' and 'His Presence is Our Priority'. The Father Says Today is a powerful breakthrough resource for your life that reflects their passion to ignite a relevant prophetic culture in the earth.

(For more information or to connect with Prophets Russ and Kitty visit www.fathersheartministry.net)